D1526144

Two Cheers for Anarchism

Two Cheers for Anarchism

Six Easy Pieces
on Autonomy,
Dignity,
and Meaningful
Work and Play

JAMES C. SCOTT

Princeton University Press

Princeton & Oxford

Copyright © 2012 by Princeton University Press

Published by Princeton University Press, 41 William Street,
Princeton, New Jersey 08540

In the United Kingdom: Princeton University Press, 6 Oxford Street,
Woodstock, Oxfordshire OX20 1TW

press.princeton.edu

LIBRARY OF CONGRESS CATALOGING-IN-PUBLICATION DATA

Scott, James C.

Two cheers for anarchism : six easy pieces on autonomy, dignity, and
meaningful work and play / James C. Scott.

p.   cm.

Includes bibliographical references and index.

ISBN 978-0-691-15529-6 (hardcover : alk. paper) 1. Anarchism. I.
Title.

HX826.S35 2012

335.83—dc23   2012015029

British Library Cataloging-in-Publication Data is available

This book has been composed in Garamond Pro

Printed on acid-free paper. ∞

Printed in the United States of America

1 3 5 7 9 10 8 6 4 2

Contents

Illustrations

Preface

The arguments found here have been gestating for a long time, as I wrote about peasants, class conflict, resistance, development projects, and marginal peoples in the hills of Southeast Asia. Again and again over three decades, I found myself having said something in a seminar discussion or having written something and then catching myself thinking, "Now, that sounds like what an anarchist would argue." In geometry, two points make a line; but when the third, fourth, and fifth points all fall on the same line, then the coincidence is hard to ignore. Struck by that coincidence, I decided it was time to read the anarchist classics and the histories of anarchist movements. To that end, I taught a large undergraduate lecture course on anarchism in an effort to educate myself and perhaps work out my relationship to anarchism. The result, having sat on the back burner for the better part of twenty years after the course ended, is assembled here.

My interest in the anarchist critique of the state was born of disillusionment and dashed hopes in revolutionary change. This was a common enough experience for those who came to political consciousness in the 1960s in North America. For me and many others, the 1960s were the high tide of what one might call a romance with peasant wars of national liberation. I was, for a time, fully swept up in this moment of utopian possibilities. I followed with some awe and, in retrospect, a great deal of naiveté the referendum for independence in Ahmed Sékou Touré's Guinea, the pan-African initiatives of Ghana's president, Kwame Nkrumah, the early elections in Indonesia, the independence and first elections in Burma, where I had spent a year, and, of course, the land reforms in revolutionary China and nationwide elections in India.

The disillusionment was propelled by two processes: historical inquiry and current events. It dawned on me, as it should have earlier, that virtually every major successful revolution ended by creating a state more powerful than the one it overthrew, a state that in turn was able to extract more resources from and exercise more control over the very populations it was designed to serve. Here, the anarchist critique of Marx and, especially, of Lenin seemed prescient. The French Revolution led to the Thermadorian Reaction, and then to the precocious and belligerent Napoleonic state. The October Revolution in Russia led to Lenin's dictatorship of the vanguard party and then to the repression of striking seamen and workers (the proletariat!) at Kronstadt, collectivization, and the gulag. If the ancien régime had presided over feudal inequality with brutality, the record of the revolutions made for similarly melancholy reading. The popular aspirations that provided the energy and courage for the revolutionary victory were, in any long view, almost inevitably betrayed.

Current events were no less disquieting when it came to what contemporary revolutions meant for the largest class in world history, the peasantry. The Viet Minh, rulers in the northern half of Vietnam following the Geneva Accords of

1954, had ruthlessly suppressed a popular rebellion of small-holders and petty landlords in the very areas that were the historical hotbeds of peasant radicalism. In China, it had become clear that the Great Leap Forward, during which Mao, his critics silenced, forced millions of peasants into large agrarian communes and dining halls, was having catastrophic results. Scholars and statisticians still argue about the human toll between 1958 and 1962, but it is unlikely to be less than 35 million people. While the human toll of the Great Leap Forward was being recognized, ominous news of starvation and executions in Kampuchea under the Khmer Rouge completed the picture of peasant revolutions gone lethally awry.

It was not as if the Western bloc and its Cold War policies in poor nations offered an edifying alternative to "real existing socialism." Regimes and states that presided dictatorially over crushing inequalities were welcomed as allies in the struggle against communism. Those familiar with this period will recall that it also represented the early high tide of development studies and the new field of development economics. If revolutionary elites imagined vast projects of social engineering in a collectivist vein, development specialists were no less certain of their ability to deliver economic growth by hierarchically engineering property forms, investing in physical infrastructure, and promoting cashcropping and markets for land, generally strengthening the state and amplifying inequalities. The "free world," especially in the Global South seemed vulnerable to both the socialist critique of capitalist inequality *and* the communist and anarchist critiques of the state as the guarantor of these inequalities.

This twin disillusionment seemed to me to bear out the adage of Mikhail Bakunin: "Freedom without socialism is privilege and injustice; socialism without freedom is slavery and brutality."

An Anarchist Squint, or Seeing Like an Anarchist

Lacking a comprehensive anarchist worldview and philosophy, and in any case wary of nomothetic ways of seeing, I am making a case for a sort of anarchist squint. What I aim to show is that if you put on anarchist glasses and look at the history of popular movements, revolutions, ordinary politics, and the state from that angle, certain insights will appear that are obscured from almost any other angle. It will also become apparent that anarchist principles are active in the aspirations and political action of people who have never heard of anarchism or anarchist philosophy. One thing that heaves into view, I believe, is what Pierre-Joseph Proudhon had in mind when he first used the term "anarchism," namely, mutuality, or *cooperation without hierarchy or state rule*. Another is the anarchist tolerance for confusion and improvisation that accompanies social learning, and confidence in spontaneous cooperation and reciprocity. Here Rosa Luxemburg's preference, in the long run, for the honest mistakes of the working class over the wisdom of the executive decisions of a handful of vanguard party elites is indicative of this stance. My claim, then, is fairly modest. These glasses, I think, offer a sharper image and better depth of field than most of the alternatives.

In proposing a "process-oriented" anarchist view, or what might be termed anarchism as praxis, the reader might reasonably ask, given the many varieties of anarchism available, what particular glasses I propose to wear.

My anarchist squint involves a defense of politics, conflict, and debate, and the perpetual uncertainty and learning they entail. This means that I reject the major stream of utopian scientism that dominated much of anarchist thought around the turn of the twentieth century. In light of the huge strides in industry, chemistry, medicine, engineering, and transportation, it was no wonder that high modernist optimism on the right and the left led to the belief that the problem of scarcity had, in principle, been solved. Scientific progress, many believed, had uncovered the laws of nature, and with them the means to solve the problems of subsistence, social organization, and institutional design on a scientific basis. As men became more rational and knowledgeable, science would tell us how we should live, and politics would no longer be necessary. Figures as disparate as the comte de Saint-Simon, J. S. Mill, Marx, and Lenin were inclined to see a coming world in which enlightened specialists would govern according to scientific principles and "the administration of things" would replace politics. Lenin saw in the remarkable total mobilization of the German economy in World War I a vision of the smoothly humming machine of the socialist future; one had only to replace the German militarists at the helm of state with the vanguard party of the proletariat, and administration would make politics beside the point. For many anarchists the same vision of progress pointed the way toward an economy in which the state was beside the point. Not only have we subsequently learned both that material plenty, far from banishing politics, creates new spheres of political struggle but also that statist socialism was less "the administration of" things than the trade union of the ruling class protecting its privileges.

Unlike many anarchist thinkers, I do not believe that the state is everywhere and always the enemy of freedom. Americans need only recall the scene of the federalized National Guard leading black children to school through a menacing crowd of angry whites in Little Rock, Arkansas, in 1957 to realize that the state can, *in some circumstances*, play an emancipatory role. I believe that even this possibility has arisen only as a result of the establishment of democratic citizenship and popular suffrage by the French Revolution, subsequently extended to women, domestics, and minorities. That means that of the roughly five-thousand-year history of states, only in the last two centuries or so has even the *possibility* arisen that states might occasionally enlarge the realm of human freedom. The conditions under which such possibilities are occasionally realized, I believe, occur only when massive extra-institutional disruption from below threatens the whole political edifice. Even this achievement is fraught with melancholy, inasmuch as the French Revolution also marked the moment when the state won direct, unmediated access to the citizen and when universal conscription and total warfare became possible as well.

Nor do I believe that the state is the only institution that endangers freedom. To assert so would be to ignore a long and deep history of pre-state slavery, property in women, warfare, and bondage. It is one thing to disagree utterly with Hobbes about the nature of society before the existence of the state (nasty, brutish, and short) and another to believe that "the state of nature" was an unbroken landscape of communal property, cooperation, and peace.

The last strand of anarchist thought I definitely wish to distance myself from is the sort of libertarianism that tolerates (or even encourages) great differences in wealth, property, and status. Freedom and (small "d") democracy are, in conditions of rampant inequality, a cruel sham as Bakunin understood. There is no authentic freedom where huge differences make voluntary agreements or exchanges nothing more than legalized plunder. Consider, for example, the case of interwar China, when famine and war made starvation common. Many women faced the stark choice of either starving or selling their children and living. For a market fundamentalist, selling a child is, after all, a voluntary choice, and therefore an act of freedom, the terms of which are valid (*pacta sunt servanda*). The logic, of course, is monstrous. It is the coercive structure of the situation in this case that impels people into such catastrophic choices.

I have chosen a morally loaded example, but one not all that uncommon today. The international trade in body parts and infants is a case in point. Picture a time-lapse photograph of the globe tracing the worldwide movement of kidneys, corneas, hearts, bone marrow, lungs, and babies. They all move inexorably from the poorest nations of the globe, and from the poorest classes within them, largely to the rich nations of the North Atlantic and the most privileged within them. Jonathan Swift's "Modest Proposal" was not far off the mark. Can anyone doubt that this trade in precious goods is an artifact of a huge and essentially coercive imbalance of life chances in the world, what some have called, entirely appropriately, in my view, "structural violence"?

The point is simply that huge disparities in wealth, property, and status make a mockery of freedom. The consolidation of wealth and power over the past forty years in the United States, mimicked more recently in many states in the Global South following neoliberal policies, has created a situation that the anarchists foresaw. Cumulative inequalities in access to political influence via sheer economic muscle, huge (state-like) oligopolies, media control, campaign contributions, the shaping of legislation (right down to designated loopholes), redistricting, access to legal knowledge, and the like have allowed elections and legislation to serve largely to amplify existing inequalities. It is hard to see any plausible way in which such self-reinforcing inequalities could be reduced through existing institutions, in particular since even the recent and severe capitalist crisis beginning in 2008 failed to produce anything like Roosevelt's New Deal. Democratic institutions have, to a great extent, become commodities themselves, offered up for auction to the highest bidder.

The market measures influence in dollars, while a democracy, in principle, measures votes. In practice, at some level of inequality, the dollars infect and overwhelm the votes. Reasonable people can disagree about the levels of inequality that a democracy can tolerate without becoming an utter charade. My judgment is that we have been in the "charade zone" for quite some time. What is clear to anyone except a market fundamentalist (of the sort who would ethically condone a citizen's selling himself—voluntarily, of course—as a chattel slave) is that democracy is a cruel hoax without *relative* equality. This, of course, is the great dilemma for an anarchist. If relative equality is a necessary condition of mutuality and freedom, how can it be guaranteed except through the state? Facing this conundrum, I believe that both theoretically and practically, the abolition of the state is not an option. We are stuck, alas, with Leviathan, though not at all for the reasons Hobbes had supposed, and the challenge is to tame it. That challenge may well be beyond our reach.

The Paradox of Organization

Much of what anarchism has to teach us concerns how political change, both reformist and revolutionary, actually happens, how we should understand what is "political," and finally how we ought to go about studying politics.

Organizations, contrary to the usual view, do not generally precipitate protest movements. In fact, it is more nearly correct to say that protest movements precipitate organizations, which in turn usually attempt to tame protest and turn it into institutional channels. So far as system-threatening protests are concerned, formal organizations are more an impediment than a facilitator. It is a great paradox of democratic change, though not so surprising from behind an anarchist squint, that the very institutions designed to avoid popular tumults and make peaceful, orderly legislative change possible have generally failed to deliver. This is in large part because existing state institutions are both sclerotic and at the service of dominant interests, as are the vast majority of formal organizations that represent established interests. The latter have a chokehold on state power and institutionalized access to it.

Episodes of structural change, therefore, tend to occur only when massive, noninstitutionalized disruption in the form of riots, attacks on property, unruly demonstrations, theft, arson, and open defiance threatens established institutions. Such disruption is virtually never encouraged, let alone initiated, even by left-wing organizations that are structurally inclined to favor orderly demands, demonstrations, and strikes that can usually be contained within the existing institutional framework. Opposition institutions with names, office bearers, constitutions, banners, and their own internal governmental routines favor, naturally enough, institutionalized conflict, at which they are specialists.[1]

As Frances Fox Piven and Richard A. Cloward have convincingly shown for the Great Depression in the United States, protests by unemployed and workers in the 1930s, the civil rights movement, the anti–Vietnam War movement, and the welfare rights movement, what success the movements enjoyed was at their most disruptive, most confrontational, least organized, and least hierarchical.[2] It was the effort to stem the contagion of a spreading, noninstitutionalized challenge to the existing order that prompted concessions. There were no leaders to negotiate a deal with, no one who could promise to get people off the streets in return for concessions. Mass defiance, precisely because it threatens the institutional order, gives rise to organizations that try to channel that defiance into the flow of normal politics, where it can be contained. In such circumstances, elites turn to organizations they would normally disdain, an example being Premier Georges Pompidou's deal with the French Communist Party (an established "player") promising huge wage concessions in 1968 in order to split the party loyalists off from students and wildcat strikers.

Disruption comes in many wondrous forms, and it seems useful to distinguish them by how articulate they are and whether or not they lay claim to the moral high ground of democratic politics. Thus, disruption aimed at realizing or expanding democratic freedoms—such as abolition, women's suffrage, or desegregation—articulate a specific claim to occupy the high ground of democratic rights. What about massive disruptions aimed at achieving the eight-hour workday or the withdrawal of troops from Vietnam, or, more nebulous, opposition to neoliberal globalization? Here the objective is still reasonably articulated but the claim to the moral high ground is more sharply contested. Though one may deplore the strategy of the "black bloc" during the "Battle in Seattle" around the World Trade Organization meeting in 1999, smashing storefronts and skirmishing with the police, there is little doubt that without the media attention their quasi-calculated rampage drew, the wider antiglobalization, anti-WTO, anti–International Monetary Fund, anti–World Bank movement would have gone largely unnoticed.

The hardest case, but one increasingly common among marginalized communities, is the generalized riot, often with looting, that is more an inchoate cry of anger and alienation with no coherent demand or claim. Precisely because it is so inarticulate and arises among the least organized sectors of society, it appears more menacing; there is no particular demand to address, nor are there any obvious leaders with whom to negotiate. Governing elites confront a spectrum of options. In the urban riots in Britain in the late summer of 2011, the Tory government's first response was repression and summary justice. Another political response, urged by Labour figures, was a mixture of urban social reform, economic amelioration, and selective punishment. What the riots undeniably did, however, was get the attention of elites, without which most of the issues underlying the riots would not have been raised to public consciousness, *no matter how they were disposed of.*

Here again there is a dilemma. Massive disruption and defiance can, under some conditions, lead directly to authoritarianism or fascism rather than reform or revolution. That is always the danger, but it is nonetheless true that extra-institutional protest seems a necessary, though not sufficient, condition for major progressive structural change such as the New Deal or civil rights.

Just as much of the politics that has historically mattered has taken the form of unruly defiance, it is also the case that for subordinate classes, for most of their history, politics has taken a very different extra-institutional form. For the peasantry and much of the early working class historically, we may look in vain for formal organizations and public manifestations. There is a whole realm of what I have called "infrapolitics" because it is practiced outside the visible spectrum of what usually passes for political activity. The state has historically thwarted lower-class organization, let alone public defiance. For subordinate groups, such politics is dangerous. They have, by and large, understood, as have guerrillas, that divisibility, small numbers, and dispersion help them avoid reprisal.

By infrapolitics I have in mind such acts as foot-dragging, poaching, pilfering, dissimulation, sabotage, desertion, absenteeism, squatting, and flight. Why risk getting shot for a failed mutiny when desertion will do just as well? Why risk an open land invasion when squatting will secure de facto land rights? Why openly petition for rights to wood, fish, and game when poaching will accomplish the same purpose quietly? In many cases these forms of de facto self-help flourish and are sustained by deeply held collective opinions about conscription, unjust wars, and rights to land and nature that cannot safely be ventured openly. And yet the accumulation of thousands or even millions of such petty acts can have massive effects on warfare, land rights, taxes, and property relations. The large-mesh net political scientists and most historians use to troll for political activity utterly misses the fact that most subordinate classes have historically not had the luxury of open political organization. That has not prevented them from working microscopically, cooperatively, complicitly, and massively at political change from below. As Milovan Djilas noted long ago,

> The slow, unproductive work of disinterested millions, together with the prevention of all work not considered "socialist", is the incalculable, invisible, and gigantic waste which no communist regime has been able to avoid.[3]

Who can say precisely what role such expressions of disaffection (as captured in the popular slogan, "We pretend to work and they pretend to pay us") played in the long-run viability of Soviet bloc economies?

Forms of informal cooperation, coordination, and action that embody mutuality without hierarchy are the quotidian experience of most people. Only occasionally do they embody implicit or explicit opposition to state law and institutions. Most villages and neighborhoods function precisely because of the informal, transient networks of coordination that do not require formal organization, let alone hierarchy. In other words, the experience of anarchistic mutuality is ubiquitous. As Colin Ward notes, "far from being a speculative vision of a future society, it is a description of a mode of human experience of everyday life, which operates side-by-side with, and in spite of, the dominant authoritarian trends of our society."[4]

The big question, and one to which I do not have a definitive answer, is whether the existence, power, and reach of the state over the past several centuries have sapped the *independent, self-organizing* power of individuals and small communities. So many functions that were once accomplished by mutuality among equals and informal coordination are now state organized or state supervised. As Proudhon, anticipating Foucault, famously put it,

To be ruled is to be kept an eye on, inspected, spied on, regulated, indoctrinated, sermonized, listed and checked off, estimated, appraised, censured, ordered about by creatures without knowledge and without virtues. To be ruled is at every operation, transaction, movement, to be noted, registered, counted, priced, admonished, prevented, reformed, redressed, corrected.[5]

To what extent has the hegemony of the state and of formal, hierarchical organizations undermined the capacity for and the practice of mutuality and cooperation that have historically created order without the state? To what degree have the growing reach of the state and the assumptions behind action in a liberal economy actually produced the asocial egoists that Hobbes thought Leviathan was designed to tame? One could argue that the formal order of the liberal state depends fundamentally on a social capital of habits of mutuality and cooperation that antedate it, which it cannot create and which, in fact, it undermines. The state, arguably, destroys the natural initiative and responsibility that arise from voluntary cooperation. Further, the neoliberal celebration of the individual maximizer over society, of individual freehold property over common property, of the treatment of land (nature) and labor (human work life) as market commodities, and of monetary commensuration in, say, cost-benefit analysis (e.g., shadow pricing for the value of a sunset or an endangered view) all encourage habits of social calculation that smack of social Darwinism.

I am suggesting that two centuries of a strong state and liberal economies may have socialized us so that we have largely lost the habits of mutuality and are in danger now of becoming precisely the dangerous predators that Hobbes thought populated the state of nature. Leviathan may have given birth to its own justification.

An Anarchist Squint at the Practice of Social Science

The populist tendency of anarchist thought, with its belief in the possibilities of autonomy, self-organization, and cooperation, recognized, among other things, that peasants, artisans, and workers were themselves political thinkers. They had their own purposes, values, and practices, which any political system ignored at its peril. That basic respect for the agency of nonelites seems to have been betrayed not only by states but also by the practice of social science. It is common to ascribe to elites particular values, a sense of history, aesthetic tastes, even rudiments of a political philosophy. The political analysis of nonelites, by contrast, is often conducted, as it were, behind their backs. Their "politics" is read off their statistical profile: from such "facts" as their income, occupation, years of schooling, property holding, residence, race, ethnicity, and religion.

This is a practice that most social scientists would never judge remotely adequate to the study of elites. It is curiously akin both to state routines and to left-wing authoritarianism in treating the nonelite public and "masses" as ciphers of their socioeconomic characteristics, most of whose needs and worldview can be understood as a vector sum of incoming calories, cash, work routines, consumption patterns, and past voting behavior. It is not that such factors are not germane. What is inadmissible, both morally and scientifically, is the hubris that pretends to understand the behavior of human agents without for a moment listening systematically to how they understand what they are doing and how they explain themselves. Again, it is not that such self-explanations are transparent and nor are they without strategic omissions and ulterior motives—they are no more transparent that the self-explanations of elites.

The job of social science, as I see it, is to provide, provisionally, the best explanation of behavior on the basis of all the evidence available, including especially the explanations of the purposive, deliberating agents whose behavior is being scrutinized. The notion that the agent's view of the situation is irrelevant to this explanation is preposterous. Valid knowledge of the agent's situation is simply inconceivable without it. No one has put the case better for the phenomenology of human action than John Dunn:

> If we wish to understand other people and propose to claim that we have in fact done so, it is both imprudent and rude not to attend to what they say. . . . What we cannot properly do is to claim to *know* that we understand him [an agent] or his action better than he does himself without access to the best descriptions which he is able to offer.[6]

Anything else amounts to committing a social science crime behind the backs of history's actors.

A Caution or Two

The use of the term "fragments" within the chapters is intended to alert the reader to what not to expect. "Fragments" is meant here in a sense more akin to "fragmentary." These fragments of text are not like all the shards of a once intact pot that has been thrown to the ground or the pieces of a jigsaw puzzle that, when reassembled, will restore the vase or tableau to its original, whole condition. I do not, alas, have an elaborately worked-out argument for anarchism that would amount to an internally consistent political philosophy starting from first principles that might be compared, say, with that of Prince Kropotkin or Isaiah Berlin, let alone John Locke or Karl Marx. If the test for calling myself an anarchist thinker is having that level of ideological rigor, then I would surely fail it. What I do have and offer here is a series of aperçus that seem to me to add up to an endorsement of much that anarchist thinkers have had to say about the state, about revolution, and about equality.

Neither is this book an examination of anarchist thinkers or anarchist movements, however enlightening that might potentially be. Thus the reader will not find a detailed examination of, say, Proudhon, Bakunin, Malatesta, Sismondi, Tolstoy, Rocker, Tocqueville, or Landauer, though I have consulted the writing of most theorists of anarchy. Nor, again, will the reader find an account of anarchist or quasi-anarchist movements: of, say, Solidarność in Poland, the anarchists of Civil War Spain, or the anarchist workers of Argentina, Italy, or France—though I have read as much as I could about "real existing anarchism" as about its major theorists.

"Fragments" has a second sense as well. It represents, for me at any rate, something of an experiment in style and presentation. My two previous books (*Seeing Like a State* and *The Art of Not Being Governed*) were constructed more or less like elaborate and heavy siege engines in some Monty Python send-up of medieval warfare. I worked from outlines and diagrams on many sixteen-foot rolls of paper with thousands of minute notations to references. When I happened to mention to Alan MacFarlane that I was unhappy with my ponderous writing habits, he put me on to the techniques of essayist Lafcadio Hearn and a more intuitive, free form of composition that begins like a conversation, starting with the most arresting or gripping kernel of an argument and then elaborating, more or less organically, on that kernel. I have tried, with far fewer ritual bows to social science formulas than is customary, even for my idiosyncratic style, to follow his advice in the hope that it would prove more reader-friendly—surely something to aim for in a book with an anarchist bent.

Two Cheers for Anarchism

ONE

The Uses of Disorder and "Charisma"

FRAGMENT 1
Scott's Law of Anarchist Calisthenics

I invented this law in Neubrandenburg, Germany, in the late summer of 1990.

In an effort to improve my barely existing German-language skills before spending a year in Berlin as a guest of the Wissenschaftskolleg, I hit on the idea of finding work on a farm rather than attending daily classes with pimply teenagers at a Goethe Institut center. Since the Wall had come down only a year earlier, I wondered whether I might be able to find a six-week summer job on a collective farm (landwirtschaftliche Produktionsgenossenschaft, or LPG), recently styled "cooperative," in eastern Germany. A friend at the Wissenschaftskolleg had, it turned out, a close relative whose brother-in-law was the head of a collective farm in the tiny village of Pletz. Though wary, the brother-in-law was willing to provide room and board in return for work and a handsome weekly rent.

As a plan for improving my German by the sink-or-swim method, it was perfect; as a plan for a pleasant and edifying farm visit, it was a nightmare. The villagers and, above all, my host were suspicious of my aims. Was I aiming to pore over the accounts of the collective farm and uncover "irregularities"? Was I an advance party for Dutch farmers, who were scouting the area for land to rent in the aftermath of the socialist bloc's collapse?

The collective farm at Pletz was a spectacular example of that collapse. Its specialization was growing "starch potatoes." They were no good for pommes frites, though pigs might eat them in a pinch; their intended use, when refined, was to provide the starch base for Eastern European cosmetics. Never had a market flatlined as quickly as the market for socialist bloc cosmetics the day after the Wall was breached. Mountain after mountain of starch potatoes lay rotting beside the rail sidings in the summer sun.

Besides wondering whether utter penury lay ahead for them and what role I might have in it, for my hosts there was the more immediate question of my frail comprehension of German and the danger it posed for their small farm. Would I let the pigs out the wrong gate and into a neighbor's field? Would I give the geese the feed intended for the bulls? Would I remember *always* to lock the door when I was working in the barn in case the Gypsies came? I had, it is true, given them more than ample cause for alarm in the first week, and they had taken to shouting at me in the vain hope we all seem to have that yelling will somehow overcome any language barrier. They managed to maintain a veneer of politeness, but the glances they exchanged at supper told me their patience was wearing thin. The aura of suspicion under which I labored, not to mention my manifest incompetence and incomprehension, was in turn getting on my nerves.

I decided, for my sanity as well as for theirs, to spend one day a week in the nearby town of Neubrandenburg. Getting there was not simple. The train didn't stop at Pletz unless you put up a flag along the tracks to indicate that a passenger was waiting and, on the way back, told the conductor that you wanted to get off at Pletz, in which case he would stop specially in the middle of the fields to let you out. Once in the town I wandered the streets, frequented cafes and bars, pretended to read German newspapers (surreptitiously consulting my little dictionary), and tried not to stick out.

The once-a-day train back from Neubrandenburg that could be made to stop at Pletz left at around ten at night. Lest I miss it and have to spend the night as a vagrant in this strange city, I made sure I was at the station at least half an hour early. Every week for six or seven weeks the same intriguing scene was played out in front of the railroad station, giving me ample time to ponder it both as observer and as participant. The idea of "anarchist calisthenics" was conceived in the course of what an anthropologist would call my participant observation.

Outside the station was a major, for Neubrandenburg at any rate, intersection. During the day there was a fairly brisk traffic of pedestrians, cars, and trucks, and a set of traffic lights to regulate it. Later in the evening, however, the vehicle traffic virtually ceased while the pedestrian traffic, if anything, swelled to take advantage of the cooler evening breeze. Regularly between 9:00 and 10:00 p.m. there would be fifty or sixty pedestrians, not a few of them tipsy, who would cross the intersection. The lights were timed, I suppose, for vehicle traffic at midday and not adjusted for the heavy evening foot traffic. Again and again, fifty or sixty people waited patiently at the corner for the light to change in their favor: four minutes, five minutes, perhaps longer. It seemed an eternity. The landscape of Neubrandenburg, on the Mecklenburg Plain, is flat as a pancake. Peering in each direction from the intersection, then, one could see a mile of so of roadway, with, typically, no traffic at all. Very occasionally a single, small Trabant made its slow, smoky way to the intersection.

Twice, perhaps, in the course of roughly five hours of my observing this scene did a pedestrian cross against the light, and then always to a chorus of scolding tongues and fingers wagging in disapproval. I too became part of the scene. If I had mangled my last exchange in German, sapping my confidence, I stood there with the rest for as long as it took for the light to change, afraid to brave the glares that awaited me if I crossed. If, more rarely, my last exchange in German had gone well and my confidence was high, I would cross against the light, thinking, to buck up my courage, that it was stupid to obey a minor law that, in this case, was so contrary to reason.

It surprised me how much I had to screw up my courage merely to cross a street against general disapproval. How little my rational convictions seemed to weigh against the pressure of their scolding. Striding out boldly into the intersection with apparent conviction made a more striking impression, perhaps, but it required more courage than I could normally muster.

As a way of justifying my conduct to myself, I began to rehearse a little discourse that I imagined delivering in perfect German. It went something like this. "You know, you and especially your grandparents could have used more of a spirit of lawbreaking. One day you will be called on to break a big law in the name of justice and rationality. Everything will depend on it. You have to be ready. How are you going to prepare for that day when it really matters? You have to stay 'in shape' so that when the big day comes you will be ready. What you need is 'anarchist calisthenics.' Every day or so break some trivial law that makes no sense, even if it's only jaywalking. Use your own head to judge whether a law is just or reasonable. That way, you'll keep trim; and when the big day comes, you'll be ready."

Judging when it makes sense to break a law requires careful thought, even in the relatively innocuous case of jaywalking. I was reminded of this when I visited a retired Dutch scholar whose work I had long admired. When I went to see him, he was an avowed Maoist and defender of the Cultural Revolution, and something of an incendiary in Dutch academic politics. He invited me to lunch at a Chinese restaurant near his apartment in the small town of Wageningen. We came to an intersection, and the light was against us. Now, Wageningen, like Neubrandenburg, is perfectly flat, and one can see for miles in all directions. There was absolutely nothing coming. Without thinking, I stepped into the street, and as I did so, Dr. Wertheim said, "James, you must wait." I protested weakly while regaining the curb, "But Dr. Wertheim, nothing is coming." "James," he replied instantly, "It would be a bad example for the children." I was both chastened and instructed. Here was a Maoist incendiary with, nevertheless, a fine-tuned, dare I say Dutch, sense of civic responsibility, while I was the Yankee cowboy heedless of the effects of my act on my fellow citizens. Now when I jaywalk I look around to see that there are no children who might be endangered by my bad example.

Toward the very end of my farm stay in Neubrandenburg, there was a more public event that raised the issue of lawbreaking in a more striking way. A little item in the local newspaper informed me that anarchists from West Germany (the country was still nearly a month from formal reunification, or *Einheit*) had been hauling a huge papier-mâché statue from city square to city square in East Germany on the back of a flatbed truck.

It was the silhouette of a running man carved into a block of granite. It was called *Monument to the Unknown Deserters of Both World Wars* (*Denkmal an die unbekannten Deserteure der beiden Weltkriege*) and bore the legend, "This is for the man who refused to kill his fellow man."

It struck me as a magnificent anarchist gesture, this contrarian play on the well-nigh universal theme of the Unknown Soldier: the obscure, "every-infantryman" who fell honorably in battle for his nation's objectives. Even in Germany, even in very recently ex–East Germany (celebrated as "The First Socialist State on German Soil"), this gesture was, however, distinctly unwelcome. For no matter how thoroughly progressive Germans may have repudiated the aims of Nazi Germany, they still bore an ungrudging admiration for the loyalty and sacrifice of its devoted soldiers. The Good Soldier Švejk, the Czech antihero who would rather have his sausage and beer near a warm fire than fight for his country, may have been a model of popular resistance to war for Bertolt Brecht, but for the city fathers of East Germany's twilight year, this papier-mâché mockery was no laughing matter. It came to rest in each town square only so long as it took for the authorities to assemble and banish it. Thus began a merry chase: from Magdeburg to Potsdam to East Berlin to Bitterfeld to Halle to Leipzig to Weimar to Karl-Marx-Stadt (Chemnitz) to Neubrandenburg to Rostock, ending finally back in the then federal capital, Bonn. The city-to-city scamper and the inevitable publicity it provoked may have been precisely what its originators had in mind.

The stunt, aided by the heady atmosphere in the two years following the breach in the Berlin Wall, was contagious. Soon, progressives and anarchists throughout Germany had created dozens of their own municipal monuments to desertion. It was no small thing that an act traditionally associated with cowards and traitors was suddenly held up as honorable and perhaps even worthy of emulation. Small wonder that Germany, which surely has paid a very high price for patriotism in the service of inhuman objectives, would have been among the first to question publicly the value of obedience and to place monuments to deserters in public squares otherwise consecrated to Martin Luther, Frederick the Great, Bismarck, Goethe, and Schiller.

A monument to desertion poses something of a conceptual and aesthetic challenge. A few of the monuments erected to deserters throughout Germany were of lasting artistic value, and one, by Hannah Stuetz Menzel, at Ulm, at least managed to suggest the contagion that such high-stakes acts of disobedience can potentially inspire (fig. 1.1).

FRAGMENT 2
On the Importance of Insubordination

Acts of disobedience are of interest to us when they are exemplary, and especially when, as examples, they set off a chain reaction, prompting others to emulate them. Then we are in the presence less of an individual act of cowardice or conscience— perhaps both—than of a social phenomenon that can have massive political effects. Multiplied many thousandfold, such petty acts of refusal may, in the end, make an utter shambles of the plans dreamed up by generals and heads of state. Such petty acts of insubordination typically make no headlines. But just as millions of anthozoan polyps create, willy-nilly, a coral reef, so do thousands upon thousands of acts of insubordination and evasion create an economic or political barrier reef of

Figure 1.1. *Memorial for the Unknown Deserter*, by Mehmet Aksoy, Potsdam. Photograph courtesy of Volker Moerbitz, Monterey Institute of International Studies

their own. A double conspiracy of silence shrouds these acts in anonymity. The perpetrators rarely seek to call attention to themselves; their safety lies in their invisibility. The officials, for their part, are reluctant to call attention to rising levels of disobedience; to do so would risk encouraging others and call attention to their fragile moral sway. The result is an oddly complicitous silence that all but expunges such forms of insubordination from the historical record.

And yet, such acts of what I have elsewhere called "everyday forms of resistance" have had enormous, often decisive, effects on the regimes, states, and armies at which they are implicitly directed. The defeat of the Confederate states in America's great Civil War can almost certainly be attributed to a vast aggregation of acts of desertion and insubordination. In the fall of 1862, little more than a year after the war began, there were widespread crop failures in the South. Soldiers, particularly those from the non-slave-holding backcountry, were getting letters from famished families urging them to return home. Many thousands did, often as whole units, taking their arms with them. Having returned to the hills, most of them actively resisted conscription for the duration of the war.

Later, following the decisive Union victory at Missionary Ridge in the winter of 1863, the writing was on the wall and the Confederate forces experienced a veritable hemorrhage of desertions, again, especially from small-holding, up-country recruits who had no direct interest in the preservation of slavery, especially when it seemed likely to cost them their own lives. Their attitude was summed up in a popular slogan of the time in the Confederacy that the war was "A rich man's war and a poor man's fight," a slogan only reinforced by the fact that rich planters with more than twenty slaves could keep one son at home, presumably to ensure labor discipline. All told, something like a quarter of a million eligible draft-age men deserted or evaded service altogether. To this blow, absorbed by a Confederacy already overmatched in manpower, must be added the substantial numbers of slaves, especially from the border states, who ran to the Union lines, many of whom then enlisted in the Union forces. Last, it seems that the remaining slave population, cheered by Union advances and reluctant to exhaust themselves to increase war production, dragged their feet whenever possible and frequently absconded as well to refuges such as the Great Dismal Swamp, along the Virginia–North Carolina border, where they could not be easily tracked. Thousands upon thousands of acts of desertion, shirking, and absconding, intended to be unobtrusive and to escape detection, amplified the manpower and industrial advantage of the Union forces and may well have been decisive in the Confederacy's ultimate defeat.

Napoleon's wars of conquest were ultimately crippled by comparable waves of disobedience. While it is claimed that Napoleon's invading soldiers brought the French Revolution to the rest of Europe in their knapsacks, it is no exaggeration to assert that the limits of these conquests were sharply etched by the disobedience of the men expected to shoulder those knapsacks. From 1794 to 1796 under the Republic, and then again from 1812 under the Napoleonic empire, the difficulty of scouring the countryside for conscripts was crippling. Families, villages, local officials, and whole cantons conspired to welcome back recruits who had fled and to conceal those who had evaded conscription altogether, some by severing one or more fingers of their right hand. The rates of draft evasion and desertion were something of a referendum on the popularity of the regime and, given their strategic importance of these "voters-with-their-feet" to the needs of Napoleon's quartermasters, the referendum was conclusive. While the citizens of the First Republic and of Napoleon's empire may have warmly embraced the promise of universal citizenship, they were less enamored of its logical twin, universal conscription.

Stepping back a moment, it's worth noticing something particular about these acts: they are virtually all anonymous, they do not shout their name. In fact, their unobtrusiveness contributed to their effectiveness. Desertion is quite different from an open mutiny that directly challenges military commanders. It makes no public claims, it issues no manifestos; it is exit rather than voice. And yet, once the extent of desertion becomes known, it constrains the ambitions of commanders, who know they may not be able to count on their conscripts. During the unpopular U.S. war in Vietnam, the reported "fragging" (throwing of a fragmentation grenade) of those officers who repeatedly exposed their men to deadly patrols was a far more dramatic and violent but nevertheless still anonymous act, meant to lessen the deadly risks of war for conscripts. One can well imagine how reports of fragging, whether true or not, might make officers hesitate to volunteer themselves and their men for dangerous missions. To my knowledge, no study has ever looked into the actual incidence of fragging, let alone the effects it may have had on the conduct and termination of the war. The complicity of silence is, in this case as well, reciprocal.

Quiet, anonymous, and often complicitous, lawbreaking and disobedience may well be the historically preferred mode of political action for peasant and subaltern classes, for whom open defiance is too dangerous. For the two centuries from roughly 1650 to 1850, poaching (of wood, game, fish, kindling, fodder) from Crown or private lands was the most popular crime in England. By "popular" I mean both the most frequent and the most heartily approved of by commoners. Since the rural population had never accepted the claim of the Crown or the nobility to "the free gifts of nature" in forests, streams, and open lands (heath, moor, open pasture), they violated those property rights en masse repeatedly, enough to make the elite claim to property rights in many areas a dead letter. And yet, this vast conflict over property rights was conducted surreptitiously from below with virtually no public declaration of war. It is as if villagers had managed, de facto, defiantly to exercise their presumed right to such lands without ever making a formal claim. It was often remarked that the local complicity was such that gamekeepers could rarely find any villager who would serve as state's witness.

In the historical struggle over property rights, the antagonists on either side of the barricades have used the weapons that most suited them. Elites, controlling the lawmaking machinery of the state, have deployed bills of enclosure, paper titles, and freehold tenure, not to mention the police, gamekeepers, forest guards, the courts, and the gibbet to establish and defend their property rights. Peasants and subaltern groups, having no access to such heavy weaponry, have instead relied on techniques such as poaching, pilfering, and squatting to contest those claims and assert their own. Unobtrusive and anonymous, like desertion, these "weapons of the weak" stand in sharp contrast to open public challenges that aim at the same objective. Thus, desertion is a lower-risk alternative to mutiny, squatting a lower-risk alternative to a land invasion, poaching a lower-risk alternative to the open assertion of rights to timber, game, or fish. For most of the world's population today, and most assuredly for subaltern classes historically, such techniques have represented the only quotidian form of politics available. When they have failed, they have given way to more desperate, open conflicts such as riots, rebellions, and insurgency. These bids for power irrupt suddenly onto the official record, leaving traces in the archives beloved of historians and sociologists who, having documents to batten on, assign them a pride of place all out of proportion to the role they would occupy in a more comprehensive account of class struggle. Quiet, unassuming, quotidian insubordination, because it usually flies below the archival radar, waves no banners, has no officeholders, writes no manifestos, and has no permanent organization, escapes notice. And that's just what the practitioners of these forms of subaltern politics have in mind: to escape notice. You could say that, historically, the goal of peasants and subaltern classes has been to stay out of the archives. When they do make an appearance, you can be pretty sure that something has gone terribly wrong.

If we were to look at the great bandwidth of subaltern politics all the way from small acts of anonymous defiance to massive popular rebellions, we would find that outbreaks of riskier open confrontation are normally preceded by an increase in the tempo of anonymous threats and acts of violence: threatening letters, arson and threats of arson, cattle maiming, sabotage and nighttime machine breaking, and so on. Local elites and officials historically knew these as the likely precursors of open rebellion; and they were intended to be read as such by those who engaged in them. Both the frequency of insubordination and its "threat level" (pace the Office of Homeland Security) were understood by contemporary elites as early warning signs of desperation and political unrest. One of the first op-eds of the young Karl Marx noted in great detail the correlation between, on the one hand, unemployment and declining wages among factory workers in the Rhineland, and on the other, the frequency of prosecution for the theft of firewood from private lands.

The sort of lawbreaking going on here is, I think, a special subspecies of collective action. It is not often recognized as such, in large part because it makes no open claims of this kind and because it is almost always self-serving at the same time. Who is to say whether the poaching hunter is more interested in a warm fire and rabbit stew than in contesting the claim of the aristocracy to the wood and the game he has just taken? It is most certainly not in his interest to help the historian with a public account of his motives. The success of his claim to wood and game lies in keeping his acts and motives shrouded. And yet, the long-run success of this lawbreaking depends on the complicity of his friends and neighbors who may believe in his and their right to forest products and may themselves poach and, in any case, will not bear witness against him or turn him in to the authorities.

One need not have an actual conspiracy to achieve the practical effects of a conspiracy. More regimes have been brought, piecemeal, to their knees by what was once called "Irish democracy," the silent, dogged resistance, withdrawal, and truculence of millions of ordinary people, than by revolutionary vanguards or rioting mobs.

FRAGMENT 3
More on Insubordination

To see how tacit coordination and lawbreaking can mimic the effects of collective action without its inconveniences and dangers, we might consider the enforcement of speed limits. Let's imagine that the speed limit for cars is 55 miles per hour. Chances are that the traffic police will not be much inclined to prosecute drivers going 56, 57, 58 . . . even 60 mph, even though it is technically a violation. This "ceded space of disobedience" is, as it were, seized and becomes occupied territory, and soon much of the traffic is moving along at roughly 60 mph. What about 61, 62, 63 mph? Drivers going just a mile or two above the de facto limit are, they reason, fairly safe. Soon the speeds from, say, 60 to 65mph bid fair to become conquered territory as well. All of the drivers, then, going about 65 mph come absolutely to depend for their relative immunity from prosecution on being surrounded by a veritable capsule of cars traveling at roughly the same speed. There is something like a contagion effect that arises from observation and tacit coordination taking place here, although there is no

"Central Committee of Drivers" meeting and plotting massive acts of civil disobedience. At some point, of course, the traffic police do intervene to issue fines and make arrests, and the pattern of their intervention sets terms of calculation that drivers must now consider when deciding how fast to drive. The pressure at the upper end of the tolerated speed, however, is always being tested by drivers in a hurry, and if, for whatever reason, enforcement lapses, the tolerated speed will expand to fill it. As with any analogy, this one must not be pushed too far. Exceeding the speed limit is largely a matter of convenience, not a matter of rights and grievances, and the dangers to speeders from the police are comparatively trivial. (If, on the contrary, we had a 55-mph speed limit and, say, only three traffic police for the whole nation, who summarily executed five or six speeders and strung them up along the interstate highways, the dynamic I have described would screech to a halt!)

I've noticed a similar pattern in the way that what begin as "shortcuts" in walking paths often end up becoming paved walkways. Imagine a pattern of daily walking trajectories that, were they confined to paved sidewalks, would oblige people to negotiate the two sides of a right triangle rather than striking out along the (unpaved) hypotenuse. Chances are, a few would venture the shortcut and, if not thwarted, establish a route that others would be tempted to take merely to save time. If the shortcut is heavily trafficked and the groundskeepers relatively tolerant, the shortcut may well, over time, come to be paved. Tacit coordination again. Of course, virtually all of the lanes in older cities that grew from smaller settlements were created in precisely this way; they were the formalization of daily pedestrian and cart tracks, from the well to the market, from the church or school to the artisan quarter—a good example of the principle attributed to Chuang Tzu, "We make the path by walking."

The movement from practice to custom to rights inscribed in law is an accepted pattern in both common and positive law. In the Anglo-American tradition, it is represented by the law of adverse possession, whereby a pattern of trespass or seizure of property, repeated continuously for a certain number of years, can be used to claim a right, which would then be legally protected. In France, a practice of trespass that could be shown to be of long standing would qualify as a custom and, once proved, would establish a right in law.

Under authoritarian rule it seems patently obvious that subjects who have no elected representatives to champion their cause and who are denied the usual means of public protest (demonstrations, strikes, organized social movement, dissident media) would have no other recourse than foot-dragging, sabotage, poaching, theft, and, ultimately, revolt. Surely the institutions of representative democracy and the freedoms of expression and assembly afforded modern citizens make such forms of dissent obsolete. After all, the core purpose of representative democracy is precisely to allow democratic majorities to realize their claims, however ambitious, in a thoroughly institutionalized fashion.

It is a cruel irony that this great promise of democracy is rarely realized in practice. Most of the great political reforms of the nineteenth and twentieth centuries have been accompanied by massive episodes of civil disobedience, riot, lawbreaking, the disruption of public order, and, at the limit, civil war. Such tumult not only accompanied dramatic political changes but was often absolutely instrumental in bringing them about. Representative institutions and elections by themselves, sadly, seem rarely to bring about major changes in the absence of the force majeure afforded by, say, an economic depression or international war. Owing to the concentration of property and wealth in liberal democracies and the privileged access to media, culture, and political influence these positional advantages afford the richest stratum, it is little wonder that, as Gramsci noted, giving the working class the vote did not translate into radical political change.[1] Ordinary parliamentary politics is noted more for its immobility than for facilitating major reforms.

We are obliged; if this assessment is broadly true, to confront the paradox of the *contribution of lawbreaking and disruption to democratic political change.* Taking the twentieth-century United States as a case in point, we can identify two major policy reform periods, the Great Depression of the 1930s and the civil rights movement of the 1960s. What is most striking about each, from this perspective, is the vital role massive disruption and threats to public order played in the process of reform.

The great policy shifts represented by the institution of unemployment compensation, massive public works projects, social security aid, and the Agricultural Adjustment Act were, to be sure, abetted by the emergency of the world depression. But the way in which the economic emergency made its political weight felt was not through statistics on income and unemployment but through rampant strikes, looting, rent boycotts, quasi-violent sieges of relief offices, and riots that put what my mother would have called "the fear of God" in business and political elites. They were thoroughly alarmed at what seemed at the time to be potentially revolutionary ferment. The ferment in question was, in the first instance, *not institutionalized.* That is to say, it was not initially shaped by political parties, trade unions, or recognizable social movements.

It represented no coherent policy agenda. Instead it was genuinely unstructured, chaotic, and full of menace to the established order. For this very reason, there was no one to bargain with, no one to credibly offer peace in return for policy changes. The menace was directly proportional to its *lack* of institutionalization. One could bargain with a trade union or a progressive reform movement, institutions that were geared into the institutional machinery. A strike was one thing, a wildcat strike was another: even the union bosses couldn't call off a wildcat strike. A demonstration, even a massive one, with leaders was one thing, a rioting mob was another. There were no coherent demands, no one to talk to.

The ultimate source of the massive spontaneous militancy and disruption that threatened public order lay in the radical increase in unemployment and the collapse of wage rates for those lucky enough still to be employed. The normal conditions that sustained routine politics suddenly evaporated. Neither the routines of governance nor the routines of institutionalized opposition and representation made much sense. At the individual level, the deroutinization took the form of vagrancy, crime, and vandalism. Collectively, it took the form of spontaneous defiance in riots, factory occupations, violent strikes, and tumultuous demonstrations. What made the rush of reforms possible were the social forces unleashed by the Depression, which seemed beyond the ability of political elites, property owners, *and, it should be noted*, trade unions and left-wing parties to master. The hand of the elites was forced.

An astute colleague of mine once observed that liberal democracies in the West were generally run for the benefit of the top, say, 20 percent of the wealth and income distribution. The trick, he added, to keeping this scheme running smoothly has been to convince, especially at election time, the next 30 to

35 percent of the income distribution to fear the poorest half more than they envy the richest 20 percent. The relative success of this scheme can be judged by the persistence of income inequality—and its recent sharpening—over more than a half century. The times when this scheme comes undone are in crisis situations when popular anger overflows its normal channels and threatens the very parameters within which routine politics operates. The brutal fact of routine, institutionalized liberal democratic politics is that the interests of the poor are largely ignored until and unless a sudden and dire crisis catapults the poor into the streets. As Martin Luther King, Jr., noted, "a riot is the language of the unheard." Large-scale disruption, riot, and spontaneous defiance have always been the most potent political recourse of the poor. Such activity is not without structure. It is structured by informal, self-organized, and transient networks of neighborhood, work, and family that lie outside the formal institutions of politics. This is structure alright, just not the kind amenable to institutionalized politics.

Perhaps the greatest failure of liberal democracies is their historical failure to successfully protect the vital economic and security interests of their less advantaged citizens through their institutions. The fact that democratic progress and renewal appear instead to depend vitally on major episodes of extra-institutional disorder is massively in contradiction to the promise of democracy as the institutionalization of peaceful change. And it is just as surely a failure of democratic political theory that it has not come to grips with the central role of crisis and institutional failure in those major episodes of social and political reform when the political system is relegitimated.

It would be wrong and, in fact, dangerous to claim that such large-scale provocations always or even generally lead to major structural reform. They may instead lead to growing repression, the restriction of civil rights, and, in extreme cases, the overthrow of representative democracy. Nevertheless, it is undeniable that most episodes of major reform have not been initiated without major disorders and the rush of elites to contain and normalize them. One may legitimately prefer the more "decorous" forms of rallies and marches that are committed to nonviolence and seek the moral high ground by appealing to law and democratic rights. Such preferences aside, structural reform has rarely been initiated by decorous and peaceful claims.

The job of trade unions, parties, and even radical social movements is precisely to institutionalize unruly protest and anger. Their function is, one might say, to try to translate anger, frustration, and pain into a coherent political program that can be the basis of policy making and legislation. They are the transmission belt between an unruly public and rule-making elites. The implicit assumption is that if they do their jobs well, not only will they be able to fashion political demands that are, in principle, digestible by legislative institutions, they will, in the process, discipline and regain control of the tumultuous crowds by plausibly representing their interests, or most of them, to the policy makers. Those policy makers negotiate with such "institutions of translation" on the premise that they command the allegiance of and hence can control the constituencies they purport to represent. In this respect, it is no exaggeration to say that organized interests of this kind are parasitic on the spontaneous defiance of those whose interests they presume to represent. It is that defiance that is, at such moments, the source of what influence they have as governing elites strive to contain and channel insurgent masses back into the run of normal politics.

Another paradox: at such moments, organized progressive interests achieve a level of visibility and influence on the basis of defiance that they neither incited nor controlled, and they achieve that influence on the presumption they will then be able to discipline enough of that insurgent mass to reclaim it for politics as usual. If they are successful, of course, the paradox deepens, since as the disruption on which they rose to influence subsides, so does their capacity to affect policy.

The civil rights movement in the 1960s and the speed with which both federal voting registrars were imposed on the segregated South and the Voting Rights Act was passed largely fit the same mold. The widespread voter-registration drives, Freedom Rides, and sit-ins were the product of a great many centers of initiative and imitation. Efforts to coordinate, let alone organize, this bevy of defiance eluded many of the ad hoc bodies established for this purpose, such as the Student Non-Violent Coordinating Committee, let alone the older, mainstream civil rights organizations such as the National Association for the Advancement of Colored People, the Congress on Racial Equality, and the Southern Christian Leadership Conference. The enthusiasm, spontaneity, and creativity of the cascading social movement ran far ahead of the organizations wishing to represent, coordinate, and channel it.

Again, it was the widespread disruption, caused in large part by the violent reaction of segregationist vigilantes and public authorities, that created a crisis of public order throughout much of the South. Legislation that had languished for years was suddenly rushed through Congress as John and Robert Kennedy strove to contain the growing riots and demonstrations, their resolve stiffened by the context of the Cold War propaganda war in which the violence in the south could plausibly be said to characterize a racist state. Massive disorder and violence achieved, in short order, what decades of peaceful organizing and lobbying had failed to attain.

I began this essay with the fairly banal example of crossing against the traffic lights in Neubrandenburg. The purpose was not to urge lawbreaking for its own sake, still less for the petty reason of saving a few minutes. My purpose was rather to illustrate how ingrained habits of automatic obedience could lead to a situation that, on reflection, virtually everyone would agree was absurd. Virtually all the great emancipatory movements of the past three centuries have initially confronted a legal order, not to mention police power, arrayed against them. They would scarcely have prevailed had not a handful of brave souls been willing to breach those laws and customs (e.g., through sit-ins, demonstrations, and mass violations of passed laws). Their disruptive actions, fueled by indignation, frustration, and rage, made it abundantly clear that their claims could not be met within the existing institutional and legal parameters. Thus, immanent in their willingness to break the law was not so much a desire to sow chaos as a compulsion to instate a more just legal order. To the extent that our current rule of law is more capacious and emancipatory than its predecessors were, we owe much of that gain to lawbreakers.

FRAGMENT 4
Advertisement: "Leader looking for followers, willing to follow your lead"

Riots and disruption are not the only way the unheard make their voices felt. There are certain conditions in which elites and leaders are especially attentive to what they have to say, to their likes and dislikes. Consider the case of charisma. It is common to speak of someone possessing charisma in the same way he could be said to have a hundred dollars in his pocket or a BMW in his garage. In fact, of course, charisma is a *relationship;* it depends absolutely on an audience and on culture. A charismatic performance in Spain or Afghanistan might not be even remotely charismatic in Laos or Tibet. It depends, in other words, on a response, a resonance with those witnessing the performance. And in certain circumstances elites work very hard to elicit that response, to find the right note, to harmonize their message with the wishes and tastes of their listeners and spectators. At rare moments, one can see this at work in real time. Consider the case of Martin Luther King, Jr., for certain audiences perhaps the most charismatic American public political figure of the twentieth century. Thanks to Taylor Branch's sensitive and detailed biography of King and the movement, we can actually see this searching for the right note at work in real time and in the call-and-response tradition of the African American church. I excerpt, at length, Branch's account of the speech King gave at the Holt Street YMCA in December 1955, after the conviction of Rosa Parks and on the eve of the Montgomery bus boycott:

> "We are here this evening—for serious business," he said, in even pulses, rising and then falling in pitch. When he paused, only one or two "yes" responses came up from the crowd, and they were quiet ones. It was a throng of shouters he could see, but they were waiting to see where he would take them. [*He speaks of Rosa Parks as a fine citizen.*]
> "And I think I speak with—with legal authority—not that I have any legal authority... that the law has never been totally clarified." This sentence marked King as a speaker who took care with distinctions, but it took the crowd no-

where. "Nobody can doubt the height of her character, no one can doubt the depth of her Christian commitment."

"That's right," a soft chorus answered.

"And just because she refused to get up, she was arrested," King repeated. The crowd was stirring now, following King at the speed of a medium walk.

He paused slightly longer.

"And you know, my friends, there comes a time," he cried, "when people get tired of being trampled over by the iron feet of oppression."

A flock of "Yeses" was coming back at him when suddenly the individual responses dissolved into a rising cheer and applause exploded beneath that cheer—all within the space of a second. The startling noise rolled on and on, like a wave that refused to break, and just when it seemed that the roar must finally weaken, a wall of sound came in from the enormous crowd outdoors to push the volume still higher. Thunder seemed to be added to the lower register— the sound of feet stomping on the wooden floor—until the loudness became something that was not so much heard as sensed by vibrations in the lungs. The giant cloud of noise shook the building and refused to go away. One sentence had set it loose somehow, pushing the call-and-response of the Negro church past the din of a political rally and on to something else that King had never known before. There was a rabbit of enormous proportions in those bushes. As the noise finally fell back, King's voice rose above it to fire again. "There comes a time, my friends, when people get tired of being thrown across the abyss of humiliation, when they experience the bleakness of nagging despair," he declared. "There comes a time when people get tired of getting pushed out of the glittering sunlight of life's July, and left standing amidst the piercing chill of an Alpine November. There—" King was making a new run, but the crowd drowned him out. No one could tell whether the roar came in response to the nerve he had touched or simply out of pride in the speaker from whose tongue such rhetoric rolled so easily. "We are here—we are here because we are tired now," King repeated [fig. 1.2].[3]

The pattern Branch so vividly depicts here is repeated in the rest of this particular speech and in most of King's speeches. Charisma is a kind of perfect pitch. King develops a number of themes and a repertoire of metaphors for expressing them. When he senses a powerful response he repeats the theme in a slightly different way to sustain the enthusiasm and elaborate it. As impressive as his rhetorical creativity is, it is utterly dependent on finding the right pitch that will resonate with the deepest emotions and desires of his listeners. If we take a long view of King as a spokesman for the black Christian community, the civil rights movement, and nonviolent resistance (each a somewhat different audience), we can see how, over time, the seemingly passive listeners to his soaring oratory helped write his speeches for him. They, by their responses, selected the themes that made the vital emotional connection, themes that King would amplify and elaborate in his unique way. The themes that resonated grew; those that elicited little response were dropped from King's repertoire. Like all charismatic acts, it was in two-part harmony.

The key condition for charisma is *listening very carefully* and responding. The condition for listening very carefully is a certain dependence on the audience, a certain relationship of power. One of the characteristics of great power is not having to listen. Those at the bottom of the heap are, in general,

Figure 1.2. Dr. Martin Luther King, Jr., delivering his last sermon, Memphis, Tennessee, April 3, 1968. Photograph from blackpast.org

better listeners than those at the top. The daily quality of the lifeworld of a slave, a serf, a sharecropper, a worker, a domestic depends greatly on an accurate reading of the mood and wishes of the powerful, whereas slave owners, landlords, and bosses can often ignore the wishes of their subordinates. The structural conditions that encourage such attentiveness are therefore the key to this relationship. For King, the attentiveness was built into being asked to lead the Montgomery bus boycott and being dependent on the enthusiastic participation of the black community.

To see how such counterintuitive "speechwriting" works in other contexts, let's imagine a bard in the medieval marketplace who sings and plays music for a living. Let's assume also, for purposes of illustration, that the bard in question is a "downmarket" performer—that he plays in the poor quarters of the town and is dependent on a copper or two from many of his listeners for his daily bread. Finally, let's further imagine that the bard has a repertoire of a thousand songs and is new to the town.

My guess is that the bard will begin with a random selection of songs or perhaps the ones that were favored in the previous towns he visited. Day after day he observes the response of his listeners and the number of coppers in his hat at the end of the day. Perhaps they make requests. Over time, surely, the bard, providing only that he is self-interestedly attentive, will narrow his performance to the tunes and themes favored by his audience—certain songs will drop out of his active repertoire and others will be performed repeatedly. The audience will have, again over time, shaped his repertoire in accordance with their tastes and desires in much the way that King's audience, again over time, shaped his speeches. This rather skeletal story doesn't allow for the creativity of the bard or orator constantly trying out new themes and developing them or for the evolving tastes of the audience, but it does illustrate the essential reciprocity of charismatic leadership.

The illustrative "bard" story is not far removed from the actual experience of a Chinese student sent to the countryside during the Cultural Revolution. Being of slight build and having no obvious skills useful to villagers, he was at first deeply resented as another mouth to feed while contributing nothing to production. Short of food themselves, the villagers gave him little or nothing to eat, and he was gradually wasting away. He discovered, however, that the villagers liked to hear his late evening recitations of traditional folktales, of which he knew hundreds. To keep him reciting in the evening, they would feed him small snacks to supplement his starvation rations. His stories literally kept him alive. What's more, his repertoire, as with our mythical bard, came over time to accord with the tastes of his peasant audience. Some of his tales left them cold, and him unfed. Some tales they loved and wanted to have told again and again. He literally sang for his supper, but the villagers, as it were, called the tune. When private trade and markets were later allowed, he told tales in the district marketplace to a larger and different audience. Here, too, his repertoire accommodated itself to his new audience.[4]

Politicians, anxious for votes in tumultuous times when tried-and-true themes seem to carry little resonance, tend, like a bard or Martin Luther King, Jr., to keep their ears firmly to the ground to assess what moves the constituents whose support and enthusiasm they need. Franklin Delano Roosevelt's first campaign for the U.S. presidency, at the beginning of the Great Depression, is a striking case in point. At the outset of the campaign, Roosevelt was a rather conservative Democrat not inclined to make promises or claims that were radical. In the course of the campaign, however, which was mostly conducted at whistle-stops, owing to the candidate's paralysis, the Roosevelt standard speech evolved, becoming more radical and expansive. Roosevelt and his speechwriters worked feverishly, trying new themes, new phrasings, and new claims at whistle-stop after whistle-stop, adjusting the speech little by little, depending on the response and the particular audience. In an era of unprecedented poverty and unemployment, FDR confronted an audience that looked to him for hope and the promise of assistance, and gradually his stump speech came to embody those hopes. At the end of the campaign, his oral "platform" was far more radical than it had been at the outset. There was a real sense in which, cumulatively, the audience at the whistle-stops had written (or shall we say "selected") his speech for him. It wasn't just the speech that was transformed but Roosevelt himself, who now saw himself embodying the aspirations of millions of his desperate countrymen.

This particular form of influence from below works only in certain conditions. If the bard is hired away by the local lord to sing him praise songs in return for room and board, the repertoire would look very different. If a politician lives or dies largely by huge donations designed as much to shape public opinion as to accommodate it, he or she will pay less attention to rank-and-file supporters. A social or revolutionary movement not yet in power is likely to have better hearing than one that has come to power. The most powerful don't have to learn how to carry a tune. Or, as Kenneth Boulding put it, "the larger and more authoritarian an organization [or state], the better the chance that its top decision-makers will be operating in purely imaginative worlds."[5]

TWO

Vernacular Order, Official Order

FRAGMENT 5
Vernacular and Official Ways of "Knowing"

I live in small inland town in Connecticut called Durham, after its much larger and better-known English namesake. Whether out of nostalgia for the landscape left behind or a lack of imagination, there is scarcely a town in Connecticut that does not simply appropriate an English place-name. Native American landscape terms tend to survive only in the names of lakes and rivers, or in the name of the state itself. It is a rare colonial enterprise that does not attempt to rename the landscape as a means of asserting its ownership and making it both familiar and legible to the colonizers. In settings as disparate as Ireland, Australia, and the Palestinian West Bank, the landscape has been comprehensively renamed in an effort to smother the older vernacular terms.

Consider, by way of illustration, the vernacular and official names for roads. A road runs between my town of Durham and the coastal town of Guilford, some sixteen miles to the south. Those of us who live in Durham call this road (among ourselves) the "Guilford Road" because it tells us exactly where we'll get to if we take it. The same road at its Guilford terminus is naturally called the "Durham Road" because it tells the inhabitants of Guilford exactly where they'll get to if they take it. One imagines that those who live midway along the road call it the "Durham Road" or the "Guilford Road" depending on which way *they* are heading. That the same road has two names depending on one's location demonstrates the situational, contingent nature of vernacular naming practices; each name encodes valuable local knowledge—perhaps the most important single thing you would want to know about a road is where it leads. Vernacular practices not only produce one road with two names but many roads with the same name. Thus, the nearby towns of Killingworth, Haddam, Madison, and Meriden each have roads leading to Durham that the local inhabitants call the "Durham Road."

Now imagine the insuperable problems that this locally effective folk system would pose to an outsider requiring a unique and definitive name for each road. A state road repair crew sent to fix potholes on the "Durham Road" would have to ask, "Which Durham Road?" Thus it comes as no surprise that the road between Durham and Guilford is reincarnated on all state maps and in all official designations as "Route 77." The naming practices of the state require a synoptic view, a standardized scheme of identification generating mutually exclusive and exhaustive designations. As Route 77, the road no longer immediately conveys where it leads; the sense of Route 77 only springs into view once we spread out a road map on which all state roads are enumerated. And yet the official name can be of vital importance. If you are gravely injured in a car crash on the Durham-Guilford Road, you will want to tell the state-dispatched ambulance team unambiguously that the road on which you are in danger of bleeding to death is Route 77.

Vernacular and official naming schemes jostle one another in many contexts. Vernacular names for streets and roads encode local knowledge. Some examples are Maiden Lane (the Lane where five spinster sisters once lived and walked, single file, to church every Sunday), Cider Hill Road (the road up the hill where the orchard and cider mill once stood), and Cream Pot Road (once the site of a dairy, where neighbors bought milk, cream, and butter). At the time when the name became fixed, it was probably the most relevant and useful name for local residents, though it might be mystifying to outsiders and recent arrivals. Other road names might refer to geographic features: Mica Ridge Road, Bare Rock Road, Ball Brook Road. The sum of roads and place-names in a small place, in fact, amounts to something of a local geography and history if one is familiar with the stories, features, episodes, and family enterprises encoded within them. For local people these names are rich and meaningful; for outsiders they are frequently illegible. The nonlocal planners, tax collectors, transportation managers, ambulance dispatchers, police officers, and firefighters, however, find a higher order of synoptic legibility far preferable. Given their way, they tend to prefer grids of parallel streets, consecutively numbered (First Street, Second Street), and compass directions (Northwest First Street, Northeast Second Avenue). Washington, D.C., is a particularly stunning example of such rational planning. New York City, by contrast, is a hybrid. Below Wall Street (marking the outer wall of the original Dutch settlement), the city is "vernacular" in its tangle of street forms and names, many of them originally footpaths; above Wall Street it is an easily legible, synoptic grid city of Cartesian simplicity, with avenues and streets at right angles to one another and enumerated, with a few exceptions, consecutively. Some midwestern towns, to relieve the monotony of numbered streets, have instead named them consecutively after presidents. As a bid for legibility, it is likely to appeal only to quiz show fans, who know when to expect "Polk," "Van Buren," "Taylor," and "Cleveland" streets to pop up; as a pedagogical tool, there is something to be said for it.

Vernacular measurement is only as precise as it needs to be for the purposes at hand. It is symbolized in such expressions as a "pinch of salt," "a stone's throw," "a book of hay," "within shouting distance." And for many purposes, vernacular rules may prove more accurate than apparently more exact systems. A case in point is the advice given by Squanto to white settlers in New England about when to plant a crop new to them, maize. He reportedly told them to "plant corn when the oak leaves were the size of a squirrel's ear." An eighteenth-century farmer's almanac, by contrast, would typically advise planting, say, "after the first full moon in May," or else would specify a particular date. One imagines that the almanac publisher would have feared, above all, a killing frost, and would have erred on the side of caution. Still, the almanac advice is, in its way, rigid: What about farms near the coast as opposed to those inland? What about fields on the north side of a hill that got less sun, or farms at higher elevations? The almanac's one-size-fits-all prescription travels rather badly. Squanto's formula, on the other hand, travels well. Wherever there are squirrels and oak trees and they are observed locally, it works. The vernacular observation, it turns out, is closely correlated with ground temperature, which governs oak leafing. It is based on a close observation of the sequence of spring events that are always sequential but may be early or delayed, drawn out or rushed, whereas the almanac relies on a universal calendrical and lunar system.

FRAGMENT 6
Official Knowledge and Landscapes of Control

The order, rationality, abstractness, and synoptic legibility of certain kinds of schemes of naming, landscape, architecture, and work processes lend themselves to hierarchical power. I think of them as "landscapes of control and appropriation." To take a simple example, the nearly universal system of permanent patronymic naming did not exist anywhere in the world before states found it useful for identification. It has spread along with taxes, courts, landed property, conscription, and police work—that is, along with the development of the state. It has now been superseded by identification numbers, photography, fingerprints, and DNA testing, but it was invented as a means of supervision and control. The resulting techniques represent a general *capacity* that can be used as easily to deliver vaccinations as to round up enemies of the regime. They centralize knowledge and power, but they are utterly neutral with respect to the purposes to which they are put.

The industrial assembly line is, from this perspective, the replacement of vernacular, artisanal production by a division of labor in which only the designing engineer controls the whole labor process and the workers on the floor become substitutable "hands." It may, for some products, be more efficient than artisanal production, but there is no doubt that it always concentrates power over the work process in those who control the assembly line. The utopian management dream of perfect mechanical control was, however, unrealizable not just because trade unions intervened but also because each machine had its own particularities, and a worker who had a vernacular, local knowledge of *this* particular milling or stamping machine was valuable for that reason. Even on the line, vernacular knowledge was essential to successful production.

Where the uniformity of the product is of great concern and where much of the work can be undertaken in a setting specifically constructed for that purpose, as in the building of Henry Ford's Model T or, for that matter, the construction of a Big Mac at a McDonald's, the degree of control can be impressive. The layout, down to the minutest detail at a McDonald's franchise, is calculated to maximize control over the materials and the work process *from the center.* That is, the district supervisor who arrives for an inspection with his handy clipboard can evaluate the franchise according to a protocol that has been engineered into the design itself. The coolers are uniform and their location is prescribed. The same goes for the deep fryers, the grills, the protocol for their cleaning and maintenance, the paper wrappers, etc., etc. The platonic form of the perfect McDonald's franchise and the perfect Big Mac has been dreamed up at central headquarters and engineered into the architecture, layout, and training so that the clipboard scoring can be used to judge how close it has come to the ideal. In its immanent logic, Fordist production and the McDonald's module is, as E. F. Schumacher noted in 1973, "an offensive against the unpredictability, unpunctuality, general waywardness and cussedness of living nature, including man."[1]

It is no exaggeration, I think, to view the past three centuries as the triumph of standardized, official landscapes of control and appropriation over vernacular order. That this triumph has come in tandem with the rise of large-scale hierarchical organizations, of which the state itself is only the most striking example, is entirely logical. The list of lost vernacular orders is potentially staggering. I venture here only the beginning of such a list and invite readers, if they have the appetite, to supplement it. National standard languages have replaced local tongues. Commoditized freehold land tenure has replaced complex local land-use practices, planned communities and neighborhoods have replaced older, unplanned communities and neighborhoods, and large factories and farms have replaced artisanal production and smallholder, mixed farming. Standard naming and identification practices have replaced innumerable local naming customs. National law has replaced local common law and tradition. Large schemes of irrigation and electricity supply have replaced locally adapted irrigation systems and fuel gathering. Landscapes relatively resistant to control and appropriation have been replaced with landscapes that facilitate hierarchical coordination.

Fragment 7
The Resilience of the Vernacular

It is perfectly clear that large-scale modernist schemes of imperative coordination can, for certain purposes, be the most efficient, equitable, and satisfactory solution. Space exploration, the planning of vast transportation networks, airplane manufacture, and other necessarily large-scale endeavors may well require huge organizations minutely coordinated by a few experts. The control of epidemics or of pollution requires a center staffed by experts receiving and digesting standard information from hundreds of reporting units.

Where such schemes run into trouble, sometimes catastrophic trouble, is when they encounter a recalcitrant nature, the complexity of which they only poorly comprehend, or when they encounter a recalcitrant human nature, the complexity of which they also poorly comprehend.

The troubles that have plagued "scientific" forestry, invented in the German lands in the late eighteenth century, and some forms of plantation agriculture typify the encounter. Wanting to maximize revenue from the sale of firewood and lumber from domain forests, the originators of scientific forestry reasoned that, depending on the soil, either the Norway spruce or the Scotch pine would provide the maximum cubic meters of timber per hectare. To this end, they clear-cut mixed forests and planted a single species simultaneously and in straight rows (as with row crops). They aimed at a forest that was easy to inspect, could be felled at a given time, and would produce a uniform log from a standardized tree (the *Normalbaum*). For a while—nearly an entire century—it worked brilliantly. Then it faltered. It turned out that the first rotation had apparently profited from the accumulated soil capital of the mixed forest it had replaced without replenishment. The single-species forest was above all a veritable feast for the pests, rusts, scales, and blights that specialized in attacking the Scotch pine or the Norway spruce. A forest of trees all the same age was also far more susceptible to catastrophic storm and wind damage. In an effort to simplify the forest as a one-commodity machine, scientific forestry had radically reduced its diversity. The lack of tree species diversity was replicated at every level in this stripped-down forest: in the poverty of insect species, of birds, of mammals, of lichen, of mosses, of fungi, of flora in general. The planners had created a green desert, and nature had struck

Figure 2.1. Scientific forest, Lithuania. Photograph © Alfas Pliura

back. In little more than a century, the successors of those who had made scientific forestry famous in turn made the terms "forest death" (*Waldsterben*) and "restoration forestry" equally famous (fig. 2.1).

Henry Ford, bolstered by the success of the Model T and wealth beyond imagining, ran into much the same problem when he tried translating his success in building cars in factories to growing rubber trees in the tropics. He bought a tract of land roughly the size of Connecticut along a branch of the Amazon and set about creating Fordlandia. If successful, his plantation would have supplied enough latex to equip all his autos with tires for the foreseeable future. It proved an unmitigated disaster. In their natural habitat in the Amazon basin, rubber trees grow here and there among mixed stands of great diversity. They thrive amid this variety in part because they are far enough apart to minimize the buildup of diseases and pests that favor them in this, their native habitat. Transplanted to Southeast Asia by the Dutch and the British, rubber trees did relatively well in plantation stands precisely because they did not bring with them the full complement of pests and enemies. But concentrated as row crops in the Amazon, they succumbed in a few years to a variety of diseases and blights that even heroic and expensive efforts at triple grafting (one canopy stock grafted to another trunk stock, and both grafted to a different root stock) could not overcome.

In the contrived and man-made auto-assembly plant in River Rouge, built for a single purpose, the environment could, with difficulty, be mastered. In the Brazilian tropics, it could not. After millions had been invested, after innumerable changes in management and reformulated plans, after riots by the workforce, Henry Ford's adventure in Brazil was abandoned.

Henry Ford started with what his experts judged to be the best rubber tree and then tried to reshape the environment to suit it. Compare this logic to its mirror image: starting with the environmental givens and then selecting the cultivars that best fit a given niche. Customary practices of potato cultivation in the Andes represent a fine example of vernacular, artisanal farming. A high-altitude Andean potato farmer might cultivate as many as fifteen small parcels, some on a rotating basis. Each parcel is distinct in terms of its soil, altitude, orientation to sun and wind, moisture, slope, and history of cultivation. There is no "standard field." Choosing from among a large number of locally developed landraces, each with different and well-known characteristics, the farmer makes a series of prudent bets, planting anywhere from one cultivar to as many as a dozen in a single field. Each season is the occasion for a new round of trials, with last season's results in terms of yield, disease, prices, and response to changed plot conditions carefully weighed. These farms are market-oriented experiment stations with good yields, great adaptability, and reliability. At least as important, they are not merely producing crops; they are reproducing farmers and communities with plant-breeding skills, flexible strategies, ecological knowledge, and considerable self-confidence and autonomy.

The logic of scientific extension agriculture in the Andes is analogous to Henry Ford's Amazonian plantations. It begins with the idea of an "ideal" potato, defined largely but not entirely in terms of yield. Plant scientists then set about breeding a genotype that will most closely approximate the desired characteristics. That genotype is grown in experimental plots to determine the conditions that best allow it to flourish. The main purpose of extension work, then, to retrofit the entire environment of the farmer's field so as to realize the potential of the new genotype. This may require the application of nitrogen fertilizer, herbicides, and pesticides, special field and soil preparation, irrigation, and the timing of cultivation (planting, watering, weeding, harvesting). As one might expect, each new "ideal" cultivar usually fails within three or four years as pests and diseases gain on it, to be replaced in turn with a newer ideal potato and the cycle begins again. To the degree that it succeeds, it turns the fields into standard fields and the farmers into standard farmers, just as Henry Ford standardized the work environment and workers in River Rouge. The assembly line and the monoculture plantation each require, as a condition of their existence, the subjugation of both the vernacular artisan and of the diverse, vernacular landscape.

FRAGMENT 8
The Attractions of the Disorderly City

It turns out that it is not only plants that seem to thrive best in settings of diversity. Human nature as well seems to shun a narrow uniformity in favor of variety and diversity.

The high tide of modernist urban planning spans the first half of the twentieth century, when the triumph of civil engineering, a revolution in building techniques and materials, and the political ambitions to remake urban life combined to transform cities throughout the West. In its ambitions, it bears more than a family resemblance to scientific forestry and plantation agriculture. The emphasis was on visual order and the segregation of function. Visually, a theme to which I shall return, utopian planners favored "the sublime straight line," right angles, and sculptural regularity. When it came to spatial layout, virtually all planners favored the strict separation of different spheres of urban activity: residential housing, commercial retail space, office space, entertainment, government offices, and ceremonial space. One can easily see why this was convenient for the planners. So many retail outlets serving so many customers could be reduced to something of an algorithm requiring so many square feet per store, so many square feet of shelf space, planned transportation links, and so forth; residences required so many square feet of living space per (standardized) family, so much sunlight, so much water, so much kitchen space, so many electric outlets, so much adjacent playground space. Strict segregation of functions minimized the variables in the algorithm: it was easier to plan, easier to build, easier to maintain, easier to police, and, they thought, easier on the eye. Planning for single uses facilitated standardization, while by comparison, planning a complex, mixed-use town in these terms would have been a nightmare.

There was one problem. People tended to hate such cities and shunned them when they could. When they couldn't, they found other ways to express their despair and contempt. It is said that the postmodern era began at precisely 3 p.m. on March 16, 1972, when the award-winning Pruitt-Igoe high-rise public housing project in St. Louis was finally and officially dynamited to a heap of rubble. Its inhabitants had, in effect, reduced it to a shell. The Pruitt-Igoe buildings were merely the flagship for an entire fleet of isolated, single-use, high-rise public housing apartment blocks that seemed degrading warehouses to most of their residents and that have now largely been demolished.

At the same time that these housing projects, sailing under the banner of "slum clearance" and the elimination of "urban blight," were being constructed, they were subjected to a comprehensive and ultimately successful critique by urbanists like Jane Jacobs, who were more interested in the vernacular city: in daily urban life, and in how the city actually functioned more than in how it looked. Urban planning, like most official schemes, was characterized by a self-conscious tunnel vision. That is, it focused relentlessly on a single objective and design with a view to maximizing that objective. If the objective was growing corn, the goal became growing the most bushels per acre; if it was Model Ts, it was producing the most Model Ts for the labor and input costs; if it was health care delivery, a hospital was designed solely for efficiency in treatment; if it was the production of lumber, the forest was redesigned to be a one-commodity machine.

Jacobs understood three things that these modernist planners were utterly blind to. First, she identified the fatal assumption that in any such activity there is *only one thing going on*, and the objective of planning is to maximize the efficiency of its delivery. Unlike the planners whose algorithms depended on stipulated efficiencies—how long it took to get to work from home, how efficiently food could be delivered to the city—she understood there were a great many human purposes embedded in any human activity. Mothers or fathers pushing baby carriages may simultaneously be talking to friends, doing errands, getting a bite to eat, and looking for a book. An office worker may find lunch or a beer with co-workers the most satisfying part of the day. Second, Jacobs grasped that it was for this reason, as well as for the sheer pleasure of navigating in an animated, stimulating, and varied environment, that complex, mixed-use districts of the city were often the most desirable locations. Successful urban neighborhoods—ones that were safe, pleasant, amenity-rich, and economically viable—tended to be dense, mixed-use areas, with virtually all the urban functions concentrated and mixed higgledy-piggledy. Moreover, they were also dynamic over time. The effort to specify and freeze functions by planning fiat Jacobs termed "social taxidermy."

Finally, she explained that if one started from the "lived," vernacular city, it became clear that the effort by urban planners to turn cities into disciplined works of art of geometric, visual order was not just fundamentally misguided, it was an attack on the actual, functioning vernacular order of a successful urban neighborhood.

Looked at from this angle, the standard practice of urban planning and architecture suddenly seems very bizarre indeed. The architect and planners proceed by devising an overall vision of the building or ensemble of buildings they propose. This vision is physically represented in drawings and, typically, in an actual model of the buildings proposed. One sees in the newspapers photographs of beaming city officials and architects looking down on the successful model as if they were in helicopters, or gods. What is astounding, from a vernacular perspective, is that no one ever experiences the city from that height or angle. The presumptive ground-level experience of real pedestrians—window-shoppers, errand-runners, aimlessly strolling lovers—is left entirely out of the urban-planning equation. It is substantially as sculptural miniatures that the plans are seen, and it is hardly surprising that they should be appreciated for their visual appeal as attractive works of art: works of art that will henceforth never be seen again from that godlike vantage point, except by Superman.

This logic of modeling and miniaturization as a characteristic of official forms of order is, I think, diagnostic. The real world is messy and even dangerous. Mankind has a long history of miniaturization as a form of play, control, and manipulation. It can be seen in toy soldiers, model tanks, trucks, cars, warships and planes, dollhouses, model railroads, and so on. Such toys serve the entirely admirable purpose of letting us play with representations when the real thing is inaccessible or dangerous, or both. But miniaturization is very much a game for grown-ups, presidents, and generals as well. When the effort to transform a recalcitrant and intractable world is frustrated, elites are often tempted to retreat to miniatures, some of them quite grandiose. The effect of this retreat is to create small, relatively self-contained utopian spaces where the desired perfection might be more nearly realized. Model villages, model cities, military colonies, show projects, and demonstration farms offer politicians, administrators, and specialists a chance to create a sharply defined experimental terrain where the number of rogue variables and unknowns is minimized. The limiting case, where control is maximized but impact on the external world is minimized, is the museum or theme park. Model farms and model towns have, of course, a legitimate role as experiments where ideas about production, design, and social organization can be tested at low risk and scaled up or abandoned, depending on how they fare. Just as often, however, as with many "designer" national capitals (e.g., Washington, D.C., St. Petersburg, Dodoma, Brasilia, Islamabad, New Delhi, Abuja), they become stand-alone architectural and political statements at odds, and often purposely so, with their larger environment. The insistence on a rigid visual aesthetic at the core of the capital city tends to produce a penumbra of settlements and slums teeming with squatters, people who, as often as not, sweep the floors, cook the meals, and tend the children of the elites who work at the decorous, planned center. Order at the center is in this sense deceptive, being sustained by nonconforming and unacknowledged practices at the periphery.

FRAGMENT 9
The Chaos behind Neatness

Governing a large state is like cooking a small fish.
Tao Te Ching

The more highly planned, regulated, and formal a social or economic order is, the more likely it is to be parasitic on informal processes that the formal scheme does not recognize and without which it could not continue to exist, informal processes that the formal order cannot alone create and maintain. Here language acquisition is an instructive metaphor.

Children do not begin by learning the rules of grammar and then using these rules to construct a successful sentence. They learn to speak the way they learn to walk: by imitation, trial, error, and endless practice. The rules of grammar are the regularities that can be observed in successful speaking, they are not the cause of successful speech.

Workers have seized on the inadequacy of the rules to explain how things actually run and have exploited it to their advantage. Thus, the taxi drivers of Paris have, when they were frustrated with the municipal authorities over fees or new regulations, resorted to what is known as a *grève de zèle*. They would all, by agreement and on cue, suddenly begin to follow *all* the regulations in the *code routier*, and, as intended, this would bring traffic in Paris to a grinding halt. Knowing that traffic circulated in Paris only by a practiced and judicious disregard of many regulations, they could, merely by following the rules meticulously, bring it to a standstill. The English-language version of this procedure is often known as the "work-to-rule" strike. In an extended work-to-rule action against the Caterpillar Corporation, workers reverted to following the inefficient procedures specified by engineers, knowing that it would cost the company valuable time and quality, rather than continuing the more expeditious practices they had long ago devised on the job. The actual work process in any office, on any construction site, or on any factory floor cannot be adequately explained by the rules, however elaborate, governing it; the work gets done only because of the effective informal understandings and improvisations outside those rules.

The planned economies of the socialist bloc before the breach in the Berlin Wall in 1989 were a striking example of how rigid production norms were sustained only by informal arrangements wholly outside the official scheme. In one typical East German factory, the two most indispensable employees were not even part of the official organizational chart. One was a "jack-of-all trades" adept at devising short-term, jury-rigged solutions to keep machines running, to correct production flaws, and to make substitute spare parts. The second indispensable employee used factory funds to purchase and store desirable nonperishable goods (e.g., soap powder, quality paper, good wine, yarn, medicines, fashionable clothes) when they were available. Then, when the factory absolutely needed a machine, spare parts, or raw material not available through the plan to meet its quotas and earn its bonuses, this employee packed the hoarded goods in a Trabant and went seeking to barter them for the necessary factory supplies. Were it not for these informal arrangements, formal production would have ceased.

Like the city official peering down at the architect's proposed model of a new development site, we are all prone to the error of equating visual order with working order and visual complexity with disorder. It is a natural and, I believe, grave mistake, and one strongly associated with modernism. How dubious such an association is requires but a moment's reflection. Does it follow that more learning is taking place in a classroom with uniformed students seated at desks arranged in neat rows than in a classroom with un-uniformed students sitting on the floor or around a table? The great critic of modern urban planning, Jane Jacobs, warned that the intricate complexity of a successful mixed-use neighborhood was not, as the aesthetic of many urban planners supposed, a representation of chaos and disorder. It was, though unplanned, a highly elaborated and resilient form of order. The apparent disorder of leaves falling in the autumn, of the entrails of a rabbit, of the interior of a jet engine, of the city desk of a major newspaper is not disorder at all but rather an intricate functional order. Once its logic and purpose are grasped, it actually looks different and reflects the order of its function.

Take the design of field crops and gardens. The tendency of modern "scientific" agriculture has favored large, capital-intensive fields, with a single crop, often a hybrid or clone for maximum uniformity, grown in straight rows for easy tillage and machine harvesting. The use of fertilizers, irrigation, pesticides, and herbicides serves to make the field conditions as suitable to the single cultivar and as uniform as possible. It is a generic module of farming that travels well and actually works tolerably well for what I think of as "proletarian" production crops such as wheat, corn, cotton, and soybeans that tolerate rough handling. The effort of this agriculture to rise above, as it were, local soils, local landscape, local labor, local implements, and local weather makes it the very antithesis of vernacular agriculture. The Western vegetable garden has some, not all, of the same features. Though it contains many cultivars they are typically planted in straight rows, one cultivar to a row, and look rather like a military regiment drawn up for inspection at a parade. The geometric order is often a matter of pride. Again, there is a striking emphasis on visual regularity from above and outside.

Contrast this with, say, the indigenous field crops of tropical West Africa as encountered by British agricultural extension agents in the nineteenth century. They were shocked. Visually, the fields seemed a mess: there were two, three, and sometimes four crops crowded into the field at a time, other crops were planted in relays, small bunds—embankments—of sticks were scattered here and there, small hillocks appeared to be scattered at random. Since to a Western eye the fields were obviously a mess; the assumption was that the cultivators were themselves negligent and careless. The extension agents set about teaching them proper, "modern" agricultural techniques. It was only after roughly thirty years of frustration and failure that a Westerner thought to actually examine, scientifically, the relative merits of the two forms of cultivation under West African conditions. It turned out that the "mess" in the West African field was an agricultural system finely tuned to local conditions. The polycropping and relay cropping ensured there was ground cover to prevent erosion and capture rainfall year-round; one crop provided nutrients to another or shaded it; the bunds prevented gully erosion; cultivars were scattered to minimize pest damage and disease.

Not only were the methods sustainable, the yields compared favorably with the yields of crops grown by the Western techniques preferred by the extension agents. What the extension agents had done was erroneously to associate visual order with working order and visual disorder with inefficiency. The Westerners were in the grip of a quasi-religious faith in crop geometry, while the West Africans had worked out a highly successful system of cultivation without regard to geometry.

Edgar Anderson, a botanist interested in the history of maize in Central America, stumbled across a peasant garden in Guatemala that demonstrated how apparent visual disorder could be the key to a finely tuned working order. Walking by it on his way to the fields of maize each day, he at first took it to be an overgrown, vegetable dump heap. Only when he saw someone working in it did he realize that it was not just a garden but a brilliantly conceived garden despite, *or rather*

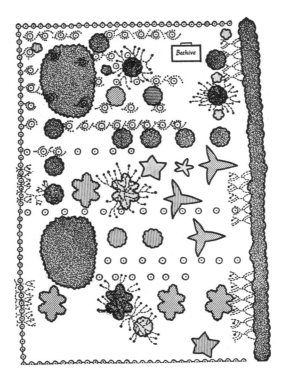

Figure 2.2.   Edgar Anderson's drawings for the Vernacular Garden, Guatemala. (a) *Above* An orchard garden. (b) *Right* Detailed glyphs identifying the plants and their categories in the garden. Reprinted from *Plants, Man, and Life*, by Edgar Anderson, published by the University of California Press; reprinted with permission of the University of California Press

because of, its visual disorder from a Western gardening perspective. I cannot do better than to quote him at length about the logic behind the garden and reproduce his diagrams of its layout (fig. 2.2).

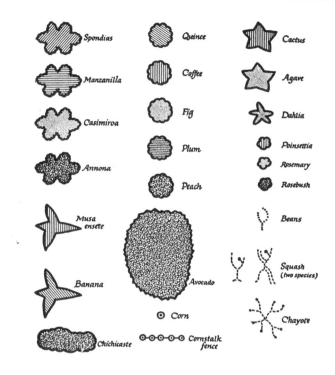

Though at first sight there seems little order; as soon as we started mapping the garden, we realized that it was planted in fairly definite cross-wise rows. There were fruit trees, native and European in great variety: annonas, cheromoyas, avocados, peaches, quinces, plums, a fig, and a few coffee bushes. There were giant cacti grown for their fruit. There was a large plant of rosemary, a plant of rue, some poinsettias, and a semi-climbing tea rose. There was a whole row of the native domesticated hawthorn, whose fruit like yellow, doll-sized apples make a delicious conserve. There were two varieties of corn, one well past bearing and now serving as a trellis for climbing string beans which were just coming into season, the other, a much taller sort, which was tasseling out. There were specimens of a little banana with smooth wide leaves which are the local substitute for wrapping paper, and are also used instead of cornhusks in cooking the native variant of hot tamales. Over it all clambered the luxuriant vines of various cucurbits. Chayote, when finally mature has a nutritious root weighing several pounds. At one point there was a depression the size of a small bathtub where a chayote root had recently been excavated; this served as a dump heap and compost for waste from the house. At one end of the garden was a small beehive made from boxes and tin cans. In terms of our American and European equivalents, the garden was a vegetable garden, an orchard, a medicinal garden, a dump heap, a compost heap, and a beeyard. There was no problem of erosion though it was at the top of a steep slope; the soil surface was practically all covered and apparently would be during most of the year. Humidity would be kept during the dry season and plants of the same sort were so isolated from one another by intervening vegetation that pests and diseases could not readily spread from plant to plant. The fertility was being conserved; in addition to the waste from the house, mature plants were being buried in between the rows when their usefulness was over.

It is frequently said by Europeans and European Americans that time means nothing to an Indian. This garden seemed to me to be a good example of how the Indian, when we look more than superficially into his activities, is budgeting time more efficiently than we do. The garden was in continuous production but was taking only a little effort at any one time: a few weeds pulled when one came down to pick the squashes, corn and bean plants dug in between the rows when the last of the climbing beans was picked, and a new crop of something else planted above them a few weeks later.[2]

FRAGMENT 10
The Anarchist's Sworn Enemy

Over the past two centuries, vernacular practices have been extinguished at such a rate that one can, with little exaggeration, think of the process as one of mass extinction akin to the accelerated disappearance of species. And the cause is also analogous: the loss of habitat. Many vernacular practices have made their final exit, and others are endangered.

The principal agent behind their extinction is none other than the anarchists' sworn enemy, the state, and in particular the modern nation-state. The rise of the modern and now hegemonic political module of the nation-state displaced and then crushed a host of vernacular political forms: stateless bands, tribes, free cities, loose confederations of towns, maroon communities, empires. In their place stands everywhere a single vernacular: the North Atlantic nation-state, codified in the eighteenth century and masquerading as a universal. It is, if we run back several hundred yards and open our eyes in wonder, nothing short of amazing that one can travel anywhere in the world and encounter virtually the same institutional order: a national flag, a national anthem, national theaters, national orchestras, heads of state, a parliament (real or fictitious), a central bank, a league table of similar ministries similarly organized, a security apparatus, and so on. Colonial empires and "modernist" emulation played a role in propagating the module, but its staying power depends on the fact that such institutions are the universal gears that integrate a political unit into the established international systems. Until 1989 there were two poles of emulation. In the socialist bloc one could go from Czechoslovakia to Mozambique, to Cuba, to Vietnam, to Laos, to Mongolia and find roughly the same central planning apparatus, collective farms, and five-year plans. Since then, with few exceptions, a single standard has prevailed.

Once in place, the modern (nation-) state set about homogenizing its population and the people's deviant, vernacular practices. Nearly everywhere, the state proceeded to fabricate a nation: France set about creating Frenchmen, Italy set about creating Italians.

This entailed a great project of homogenization. A huge variety of languages and dialects, often mutually unintelligible, were, largely through schooling, subordinated to a standardized national language—often the dialect of the dominant region. This led to the disappearance of languages; of local literatures, oral and written; of music; of legends and epics; of whole worlds of meaning. A huge variety of local laws and customary practices were replaced by a national system of law that was, in principle at least, everywhere the same. A huge variety of land-use practices were replaced by a national system of land titling, registration, and transfer, the better to facilitate taxation. A huge number of local pedagogies—apprenticeships, tutoring by traveling "masters," healing, religious instruction, informal classes—were typically replaced by a national school system in which a French minister of education could boast that, as it was 10:20 a.m., he knew exactly which passage of Cicero all students of a certain form throughout France would be studying. This utopian image of uniformity was seldom achieved, but what these projects did accomplish was the destruction of vernaculars.

Beyond the nation-state itself, the forces of standardization are today represented by international organizations. It is the principal aim of institutions such as the World Bank, the International Monetary Fund, the World Trade Organization, UNESCO, and even UNICEF and the World Court to propagate normative ("best practice") standards, once again deriving from the North Atlantic nations, throughout the globe. The financial muscle of these agencies is such that failure to conform to their recommendations carries substantial penalties in loans and aid forgone. The process of institutional alignment now goes by the charming euphemism of "harmonization." Global corporations are instrumental as well in this project of standardization. They too thrive in a familiar and homogenized cosmopolitan setting where the legal order, the commercial regulations, the currency system, and so on are uniform. They are also, through their sales of goods, services, and advertising, constantly working to fabricate consumers, whose needs and tastes are what they require.

The disappearance of some vernaculars need hardly be mourned. If the standardized model of the French citizen bequeathed to us by the Revolution replaced vernacular forms of patriarchal servitude in provincial France, then surely this was an emancipatory gain. If technical improvements like matches and washing machines replaced flint and tinder and washboards, it surely meant less drudgery. One would not want to spring to the defense of all vernaculars against all universals.

The powerful agencies of homogenization, however, are not so discriminating. They have tended to replace virtually all vernaculars with what they represent as universal, but let us recall again that in most cases it is a North Atlantic cross-dressed vernacular masquerading as a universal. The result is a massive diminution in cultural, political, and economic diversity, a massive homogenization in languages, cultures, property systems, political forms, and above all modes of sensibility and the lifeworlds that sustain them. One can look anxiously ahead to a time, not so far away, when the North Atlantic businessman can step off a plane anywhere in the world and find an institutional order—laws, commercial codes, ministries, traffic systems, property forms, land tenure—thoroughly familiar. And why not? The forms are essentially his own. Only the cuisine, the music, the dances, and native costumes will remain exotic and folkloric . . . and thoroughly commercialized as a commodity as well.

THREE

The Production of Human Beings

The great Way is very smooth
But people love by-paths.
Tao Te Ching

FRAGMENT 11
Play and Openness

In the unpromising year of 1943 in Copenhagen, the architect for a Danish workers' housing cooperative at Emdrup had a new idea for a playground. An experienced landscape architect who had laid out many conventional playgrounds, he noticed that most children were tempted to forsake the limited possibilities of the swings, seesaws, carousels, and sliding boards for the excitement in the street and to steal into actual building sites or vacant buildings and use the materials they found there for purposes they invented on the spot. His idea was to design a raw building site with clean sand, gravel, lumber, shovels, nails, and tools, and then leave it to the kids. It was hugely popular. Despite the site being crowded day after day, the possibilities were so endless and absorbing that there was far less fighting and screaming than in the classical playground.

The runaway success of the "adventure playground" at Emdrup led to efforts to emulate it elsewhere: in "Freetown" in Stockholm, "The Yard" in Minneapolis, other "building playgrounds" in Denmark itself, and "Robinson Crusoe" playgrounds in Switzerland, where children were given the tools to make their own sculptures and gardens (fig. 3.1).

"The Yard," shortly after it began, ran into trouble. Much of the lumber and many of the tools were hoarded and hidden in the competition to build the largest shack as quickly as possible. Quarreling and a number of raids to plunder tools and material broke out. It appeared, as paralysis gripped the playground, that it would now have to be taken over and run by adult park employees. But after only a few days many of the youngsters, who knew where most of the material was hoarded, organized a "salvage drive" to recover the materials and set up a system for sharing the tools and lumber. They had not only solved the practical problem of securing the material they needed but had, in doing so, created something of a new community. It should be added that this wildly popular playground satisfied the creative urges of most of the children, but it by no means satisfied the standards for visual order and decorum that the custodians of such urban spaces expected. It was a case of working order trumping visual order. And of course, its shape changed daily; it was being torn down and rebuilt continually. The adventure playground, Colin Ward, writes,

> is a kind of parable of anarchy, a free society in miniature, with the same tensions and ever-changing harmonies, the

Figure 3.1.   Playground constructions, Emdrup, Denmark. Photograph © Tim R. Gill

same diversity and spontaneity, the same unforced growth of co-operation and release of individual qualities and communal sense, which lie dormant.[1]

I recall visiting the slum housing project of an NGO in Bangkok that used essentially the same insight not only to create housing for squatters but also to build a political movement around it. The NGO began by persuading the municipality to deed it a tiny parcel of land in a squatter area. The organizers then identified no more than five or six squatter families who wanted to band together to build a tiny settlement. The squatters chose the materials, selected the basic layout, designed the structures, and agreed on a work plan together. Each family was responsible for an equal amount of sweat equity over the two- or three-year process of (spare-time) building. No family knew what section of the attached structures they would occupy when it was finished; all thus had an equal interest in the quality and care that went into each stage of the building. The squatters also designed a tiny, shared common ground that was built into the scheme. By the time the building was up, a structure of work and cooperation (not without tensions, to be sure) was already in place. Now the families had property they had built with their own hands to defend and they had, in the process, acquired the practice of working successfully together. They, and other groups like them, became the institutional nodes of a successful squatter movement.

The magnetism of the Emdrup playground, obvious in retrospect, perhaps, flowed from its openness to the purposes, creativity, and enthusiasm of the children who played there. It was deliberately incomplete and open. It was meant to be completed by the unpredictable and changing designs of its users. One could say that its designers were radically modest about their knowledge of what was on children's minds, what they would invent, how they would work, and how their hopes and dreams would evolve. Beyond the premise that children wanted to build, based on observation of what actually interested children, and that they needed the raw material to do so, the playground was open and autonomous. There was minimal adult supervision.

Almost any human institution can be evaluated in these terms. How open is it to the purposes and talents of those who inhabit it? There are only a certain number of things one can do with a swing or a seesaw, and children have explored them all! An open building site offers a veritable buffet of possibilities by comparison. Dormitory rooms of standard layout and painted the same color, with bunk beds and desks screwed to the wall or floor, are, well, closed structures that resist the impress of student imagination and design. Rooms or apartments with movable partitions, variable furniture and color schemes, and spaces that can be used for various purposes are, by comparison, more open to the inspiration of their users. In some cases it is possible to design with a view to accommodating the choices of users. A large open grassy area at a major university was deliberately left for a time without walkways. Over time, footpaths were traced by the actual daily movements of thousands of pedestrians. Those tracings were then paved to reflect what seemed required. This procedure is another illustration of Chuang Tzu's adage, "We make the path by walking."

The test of openness is the degree to which the activity or institution—its form, its purposes, its rules—can be modified by the mutual desires of the people pursuing and inhabiting it.

A brief example comparing war memorials may be helpful. The Vietnam Memorial in Washington, D.C., is surely one of the most successful war memorials ever built, if one is to judge from the quantity and intensity of the visits it receives. Designed by Maya Lin, the memorial consists simply of a gently undulating site marked (not dominated) by a long, low, black marble wall listing the names of the fallen. The names are deliberately not listed alphabetically or by military unit or rank but rather chronologically, in the order in which they fell—thus grouping those who fell on the same day and often in the same engagement. No larger claim is made about the war either in prose or in sculpture—a muteness that is not surprising, in view of the stark political cleavages the war still inspires. What is most remarkable, however, is the way the Vietnam Memorial works for those who visit it, particularly those who come to honor a comrade or loved one. They must first search out the name they seek; then they typically run their fingers over the name incised on the wall, make rubbings, and leave artifacts and mementos of their own—everything from poems, a woman's high-heeled shoe, or a glass of champagne to a full-house, aces-high, poker hand. So many of these tributes have been left that a separate museum has been created to house them. The scene of many people together at the wall, touching the names of particular loved ones who fell in the same war, has moved observers regardless of their position on the war itself.

I believe that a great part of the memorial's symbolic power is its capacity to honor the dead with an openness that allows all visitors to impress on it their own unique meanings, their own histories, their own memories. The monument, one could say, virtually requires participation to complete its meaning. Although one would not compare it to a Rorschach test, the memorial nevertheless does achieve its meaning more by what citizens bring to it than by what it imposes. (A truly cosmopolitan monument to the war would, of course, list all Vietnamese civilian and military war dead, together with Americans in the order in which they had fallen. Such a monument would require a wall many times longer than the current one.)

We may compare the Vietnam Memorial to a very different American war memorial: the sculpture depicting the raising of the American flag on the summit of Mount Suribachi on Iwo Jima in World War II. Moving in its own right, referring as it does to the final moment of a victory gained at an enormous cost in lives, the Iwo Jima statue is manifestly heroic. Its patriotism, symbolized by the flag, its theme of conquest, its larger-than-life scale, and its implicit theme of unity in victory leave little room for the viewer to add anything. Given the virtual unanimity with which that war is viewed in the United States, it is hardly surprising that the Iwo Jima Memorial should be

Figure 3.2.   Vietnam Memorial, Washington, D.C. Photograph © Lee Bennett, Jr. / www.ATPM.com

monumental and explicit. Although not exactly "canned," the Iwo Jima Memorial is more symbolically self-sufficient, as are most war memorials. Visitors can stand in awe, gazing on an image that through photographs and sculpture has become an icon of the war in the Pacific, but they receive its message rather than complete it (fig. 3.3).

The example of play invoked earlier may seem trivial by comparison with war and death. After all, play has no purpose at all beyond the pleasure and enjoyment of play itself. It is successful, even efficient, to the degree to which those who are playing judge it to be more fun than other things they might be doing. And yet play is deeply instructive, for it turns out that open, unstructured play of this kind, looked at broadly, is serious business indeed.

Figure 3.3. Iwo Jima Memorial, Washington, D.C. Photograph by Dennis @ visitingDC.com

All mammals, but especially *Homo sapiens*, appear to spend a great deal of time in apparently aimless play. Among other things, it is through the apparent chaos of play, including rough-and-tumble carousing, that they develop their physical coordination and capacities, their emotional regulation, their capacity for socialization, adaptability, their sense of belonging and social signaling, trust, and experimentation. Play's importance is revealed above all in the catastrophic effects of eliminating play from the repertoire of mammals, including *Homo sapiens sapiens*. Denied play, no mammals become successful adults. Among humans, those deprived of play are far more prone to violent antisocial behavior, depression, and pervasive distrust. The founder of the National Institute for the Study of Play, Stuart Brown, began to suspect the importance of play when he first realized that what most violently antisocial people had in common was a deep history of play deprivation. Play, along with two other major apparently purposeless human activities, sleeping and dreaming, turns out to be foundational, both socially and physically.

FRAGMENT 12
It's Ignorance, Stupid! Uncertainty and Adaptability

The concept of efficiency would appear to be at cross purposes with the openness that characterizes play. Once the purpose of an activity is sharply defined—making automobiles, paper cups, plywood sheets, or electric light bulbs—there often seems to be a single most efficient way to go about it, at least under current conditions. If the task environment of an institution or factory remains repetitive, stable, and predictable, a set of fixed routines may well prove exceptionally efficient and, perforce, closed.

This view of "efficient" is deficient in at least two respects.

First and most obvious, in most economies and human affairs generally, such static conditions are the exception rather than the rule and, when conditions change appreciably, these routines are likely to prove maladaptive. The larger the repertoire of skills a worker has and the greater her capacity to add to that repertoire, the more adaptive she is likely to be to an unpredictable task environment and, by extension, the more adaptable an institution composed of such adaptable individuals is likely to be. Adaptability and breadth serve as a personal and institutional insurance policy in the face of an uncertain environment. This was, in a larger sense, arguably the single

most important advantage *Homo erectus* had over its primate
competitors: an impressive capacity to adapt to a capricious
environment, and eventually to act on that environment.

The importance of adaptability and breadth was brought
home to me in a practical way by a brief article on nutrition in
my university's health newsletter. It noted, reasonably enough,
that scientific research had in the past decade and a half discovered a good many nutrients now understood to be essential
for good health. So far, so good. Then it made what I thought
was an original observation (which I paraphrase here). "We
expect," it went on, "that in the next decade and a half we will
uncover many new, essential elements in the diet of which we
are not now aware." "In light of this," it continued, "the best
advice we can give you is to eat the most varied diet of which
you are capable in the hope that you will have included them."
Here, then, was advice that built in the postulate of our igno-
rance about the future.

The second deficiency embedded in a static concept of efficiency is that it ignores utterly the way in which the efficiency
of any process that involves human labor depends on what
those workers will tolerate. The Lordsville, Ohio, General
Motors automobile assembly plant was, when it was built, the
absolute state of the art in terms of assembly lines. The steps
and movements in assembly had been broken down into thousands of distinct steps and was a model of Fordist efficiency.
The buildings were well lighted and ventilated, the factory
floor was kept scrupulously clean, there was piped music to
counteract the mechanical noise, rest breaks were built into
the schedule. It was also, in the name of efficiency, the fastest-
moving assembly line ever devised, requiring a tempo of work
that was without precedent. The workers resisted the line
and found ways to stop it by inconspicuous acts of sabotage.

In their frustration and anger, they damaged many parts so that the percentage of defective pieces that had to be replaced soared. Eventually the line had to be redesigned and slowed to a humane pace. For our purposes, what is crucial here is that the resistance by the workforce to its inhuman speed actually made the design inefficient. There is no such thing as labor efficiency in neoclassical economics that does not implicitly assume conditions that the workforce will accept and tolerate. If workers refuse to conform to the discipline of the work plan they can, by their own acts, nullify its efficiency.

FRAGMENT 13
GHP: The Gross Human Product

What if we were to ask a different question of institutions and activities than the narrow neoclassical question of how efficient they are in terms of costs (e.g., resources, labor, capital) per unit of a given, specified product? What if we were to ask what kind of people a given activity or institution fostered? Any activity we can imagine, any institution, no matter what its manifest purpose, is also, willy-nilly, transforming people.

What if we were to bracket the manifest purpose of an institution and the efficiency with which it is achieved and ask what the human product was? There are many ways of evaluating the human results of institutions and economic activities and it is unlikely that we could devise a convincing comprehensive measure of, say, GHP, for gross human product, that would be comparable to the economists' GDP, gross domestic product, measured in monetary units

If, undaunted by these difficulties, we decided to make a stab at it, we could, I think, identify two plausible approaches:

one that would gauge how a work process enlarged human capacities and skills and one that took its bearings from the judgments of the workers themselves about their satisfaction. The former is, at least in principle, measurable, in ordinal terms of "more or less."

What if we were to apply the standard of human capacities and skills to the industrial assembly line? After five or ten years on the assembly line at Lordsville or River Rouge, what are the odds that the capacities and skills of a worker would have been substantially enlarged? Vanishingly small, I would suspect. In fact, the whole point of the time-and-motion analysis behind the division of labor on the line was to break down the work process into thousands of minute steps that could easily be learned. It was deliberately designed to eliminate the artisanal-craft knowledge, and the power this knowledge conferred on workers, that characterized the carriage-making era. The line was premised on a deskilled, standardized workforce in which one "hand" could be easily substituted for another. It depended, in other words, on what we might legitimately call the "stupidification" of the workforce. If by chance a worker did enlarge his capacities and skills, he either did it on his own time or, perversely, by devising cunning strategies to thwart the intentions of management, as at Lordsville. Nevertheless, were we scoring assembly-line work by the degree to which it served to enlarge human capacities and skills, it would receive failing grades, no matter how efficient it was at producing cars. More than a century and a half ago, Alexis de Tocqueville, commenting on Adam Smith's classic example of the division of labor, asked the essential question: "What can be expected of a man who has spent twenty years of his life making heads for pins."[2]

In economics there is something called "Hicksian income," after the British economist John Hicks. It represented an early version of welfare economics in which Hicksian income accrued only if the factors of production, land and labor in particular, were not degraded in the process. If they were degraded, that meant that the next round of production would begin with inferior factors of production. Thus, if a technique of agricultural production depleted the soil nutrients (sometimes called "soil mining"), that loss would be reflected in a diminished Hicksian income. By the same token, any form of production such as the assembly line that degraded the talents and capacities of the workforce would, to that degree, be charged with losses in Hicksian income. The opposite also applies. Cultivation practices that systematically built up soil nutrients and tilth or manufacturing practices that expanded the skills and knowledge of the workforce would be reflected in an increment to the farmer's or firm's Hicksian income. What welfare economists term positive and negative externalities were built into the Hicksian calculus, though rarely, of course, appearing in the firm's net profit.

The term "capacities" as we have used it here could be understood narrowly or broadly. Taken narrowly with respect to, say, auto workers, it might refer to how many "positions" on the line they had held, whether they had learned pop-riveting, welding, tolerance adjustments, and so forth. Taken broadly, it might mean whether they had been trained and qualified for more skilled or management work, whether they had gained cooperative experience in the organization of the work process itself, whether their creativity was fostered, whether they had learned the skills of negotiation and representation on the job. If we were to apply the test of an enlarged capacity for democratic citizenship, it is obvious that the assembly line itself is a profoundly authoritarian environment where decisions are in the hands of the engineers and the substitutable units of the workforce are expected to do the work assigned them more or less mechanically. It never quite works out that way, but that's the imminent logic of the line. The line as a work process would have a negative "net democratic product."

What if we asked the same questions of the school, the major public institution of socialization for the young in much of the world? The query is all the more appropriate in light of the fact that the public school was invented more or less at the same time as the large factory under a single roof, and the two institutions bear a strong family resemblance. The school was, in a sense, a factory for the basic training of the minimal skills of numeracy and literacy necessary for an industrializing society. Gradgrind, the calculating, hectoring caricature of a headmaster in Charles Dickens's *Hard Times*, is meant to remind us of the factory: its work routines, its time discipline, its authoritarianism, its regimented visual order, and, not least, the demoralization and resistance of its pint-sized, juvenile workers.

Universal public education is, of course, designed to do far more than merely turn out the labor force required by industry. It is as much a political as an economic institution. It is designed to produce a patriotic citizen whose loyalty to the nation will trump regional and local identities of language, ethnicity, and religion. The universal citizenship of revolutionary France had its counterpart in universal conscription. Manufacturing such patriotic citizens through the school system was accomplished less through the manifest curriculum than through its language of instruction, its standardization, and its implicit lessons in regimentation, authority, and order.

The modern primary and secondary school system has been much altered by changing theories of pedagogy and, most especially, by affluence and the "youth culture" itself. But there is no mistaking its origins in the factory, if not the prison. Compulsory universal education, however democratizing in one sense, has also meant that, with few exceptions, the students have to be there. The fact that attendance is not a choice, not an autonomous act, means that it starts out fundamentally on the wrong foot as a compulsory institution, with all the alienation that this duress implies, especially as children grow older.

The great tragedy of the public school system, however, is that it is, by and large, a one-product factory. This tendency has only been exacerbated by the push in recent decades for standardization, measurement, testing, and accountability. The resulting incentives for students, teachers, principals, and whole school districts have had the effect of bending all efforts toward fashioning a standard product that satisfies the criteria the auditors have established.

What is this product? It is a certain form of analytical intelligence, narrowly conceived, which can, it is assumed, be measured by tests. We know, of course, that there are many, many skills that are valuable and important for a successful society that are not even remotely related to analytical intelligence, among them, artistic talent, imaginative intelligence, mechanical intelligence (the kind that Ford's early workers brought with them from the farm), musical and dance skills, creative intelligence, emotional intelligence, social skills, and ethical intelligence. Some of these aptitudes find a place in extracurricular activities, especially sports, but not in the measured and graded activities on which so much now depends for students, teachers, and schools. This monochromatic flattening of education is brought to a kind of apotheosis in educational systems like those in France, Japan, China, and Korea, where the exercise culminates in a single examination on which one's future mobility and life's chances substantially depend. Here the scramble to get into the best-regarded schools, to find extra-hours tutoring, and to attend special exam-preparation cram courses reaches a fever pitch.

How ironic it is that I, who write this, and virtually anyone who reads it, are the beneficiaries, the victors, of this rat race. It reminds me of a graffito I once saw in a Yale toilet stall. Someone had written, "Remember, even if you win the rat race, you're still a rat!" Below, in a different hand, someone else had riposted, "Yeah, but you're a winner."

Those of us who "won" this race are the lifetime beneficiaries of opportunities and privileges that would not likely otherwise have come our way. We are also are likely to carry a lifetime sense of entitlement, superiority, accomplishment, and self-esteem that comes from this victory. Let us bracket, for the moment, the question of whether this dividend is justified and what it actually means in terms of our value to ourselves and others, and merely note that it represents a fund of social capital that adjusts the odds of financial and status mobility radically in our favor. This is a lifetime privilege extended to perhaps one-fifth at most of those the system turns out.

And what of the rest? What of the, say, 80 percent who in effect lose the race? They carry less social capital; the odds are adjusted against them. Perhaps as important is the fact that they are likely to carry a lifelong sense of having been defeated, of being less valued, of thinking that they are inferior and slow-witted. This system effect further adjusts the odds against them. And yet, have we any rational reason to credit the judgments of a system that values such a narrow bandwidth of human talents and measures achievement within this band by the ability to sit successfully for an exam?

Those who do poorly on tests of analytical intelligence may be incredibly talented at one or more of the many forms of intelligence that are neither taught nor valued by the school system. What sort of a system is it that wastes these talents, that sends four-fifths of its students away with a permanent stigma in the eyes of society's gatekeepers, and perhaps in their own eyes as well? Are the dubious benefits of the privileges and opportunities accorded a presumed "analytical intelligence elite" by this pedagogical tunnel vision worth so much social damage and waste?

Fragment 14
A Caring Institution

A chilling encounter with a "caring" institution twenty years ago brought me up short. Two of my aunts, both widowed and without surviving children, were living in a retirement home in West Virginia not far from where they had taught school. It was a small retirement home for about twenty women, who were expected to dress themselves and walk under their own power to meals in the common dining room. They were in their mid-eighties, and one of them had recently sustained a fall, requiring a hospital stay that was somewhat prolonged because she had to demonstrate to the retirement home that she was up and walking before it would take her back.

Realizing that, as they became frailer, they would have to leave the retirement home and enter a convalescent home providing more intensive care, my aunts asked me, their closest relative among the next generation, to come and survey the convalescent homes so they might choose the best care they could afford.

I arrived on a Friday, and by the time we sat down to dinner at their retirement home on Saturday, I had visited two convalescent homes that seemed acceptable, though one seemed a bit friendlier and better scrubbed, with less of the smell that permeates even the best of them. Wanting to know what the residents themselves thought of each place, I had conducted something of an informal survey by going from room to room introducing myself, explaining my aunts' situation, and listening to what the residents had to say. The evaluations were very positive: they praised the care they received, the attention of the staff, the food, and the weekly activities and small outings afforded them.

I set out again on Sunday to "bag" two more convalescent homes nearby, hoping to see six in all before I had to fly back. That morning I began, as on Saturday, talking to the staff and then to the residents. On the floor nearest the reception area, there appeared to be only one nurse, who then took me around the facility, explaining things as she went. When she had finished, I said I would like to talk to a few residents, and she, knowing I was looking on behalf of my two aunts, took me first to a room shared by sisters who had arrived together the year before.

After introducing myself and explaining why I wanted to hear about their experience, I listened as they praised their care with animation and some enthusiasm. "Another suitable place," I began to think. Just then, the phone could be heard ringing faintly in the distance at the nurses' station. The nurse excused herself, explaining that they were always a bit shorthanded on Sunday, and sped down the hall to answer the phone. The moment she was well out of hearing distance, one of the sisters put her finger to her lips and with great feeling said, "Whatever you do, don't send your aunts here!" "They treat us terribly." "If we complain about anything or ask for extra help, they shout at us and tell us to shut up." They explained how some of the staff would delay bathing them or bringing their food or personal effects if they displeased them in any way. At this point, as the nurse's footsteps could be heard approaching the room, one of the sisters put her finger to her mouth again and we resumed an innocuous conversation as the nurse entered.

As I drove off to inspect a fourth convalescent home, it dawned on me that I had just witnessed the operation of a regime of low-level terror. To judge by this experience, the residents, constantly dependent on the staff for their basic needs, were afraid to say anything other than what they thought the staff expected from them, lest they be punished. My aunts, particularly the lifelong English and debate teacher with a Napoleon complex, would not fare well under this regime. I also realized that until this last incident I had always spoken with the residents with a staff member constantly at my side. Henceforth, when I visited the four additional convalescent homes on my list, I insisted that I be allowed to walk on my own through most of the facility and talk with those I met. If this request was refused, as it was in three of the four, I left immediately.

In the end, I found other grounds on which to make a choice. At one place, when I described my aunts as teachers, one head nurse asked me who they were and then exclaimed, "Oh, Miss Hutchinson! I remember her; she was my high school English teacher. She was strict, but I remember how she would invite us all out to her farm in Sandyville." It seemed to me that as long as my aunt was "Miss Hutchinson, our

English teacher," and not merely an anonymous frail person in her eighties, I had reason to hope for better and more personal care that, ideally, would extend to her roommate and sister as well. I only hoped that my Aunt Elinore's Napoleon complex was not so memorable that her student would want to make a St. Helena of her convalescence.

What was so demoralizing to me was to envision my two aunts, who had long been figures of power and authority to conjure with, reduced in the last stage of their life to such servility, fear, and silence. Nor could one ignore the infantilizing terms of address that prevailed among the overburdened staff when they spoke to their charges: "Now, dearie, it's time to take our pills like a good little girl."

It's not difficult to imagine how quickly and how thoroughly conditions of such abject bodily dependence for the most basic needs on a hard-pressed and underpaid staff might induce an "institutional personality," how infantilization might produce elderly infants. The convalescent home, not unlike the prison, the cloister, and the barracks, is something of a "total" institution of such comprehensive power that the pressures to adapt to its institutional norms are nearly irresistible.

FRAGMENT 15
Pathologies of the Institutional Life

We live most of our lives in institutions: from the family to the school, to the army, to the business enterprise. These institutions to some considerable degree shape our expectations, our personalities, and our routines. Recognizing that these institutions are varied and that they are not static, can we nevertheless say something about the aggregate effects of such institutions in shaping us?

I believe we can, in a rough-and-ready way. The first thing to notice is that since the Industrial Revolution and headlong urbanization, a vastly increasing share of the population has become propertyless and dependent on large, hierarchical organizations for their livelihood. The household economy of the small farmer-peasant or shopkeeper may have been just as poverty-stricken and insecure as that of the proletarian. It was, however, decidedly less subject to the quotidian, direct discipline of managers, bosses, and foremen. Even the tenant farmer, subject to the caprice of his landlord, or the smallholder, deeply in debt to the bank or moneylenders, was in control of his working day: when to plant, how to cultivate, when to harvest and sell, and so forth. Compare this to the factory worker tied to the clock from 8 a.m. to 5 p.m., tied to the rhythm of the machine, and closely monitored personally or electronically. Even in the service industries the pace, regulation, and monitoring of work are far beyond what the independent shopkeeper experienced in terms of minute supervision.

The second thing to notice is that these institutions are, with very few exceptions, profoundly hierarchical and, typically, authoritarian. Training, one might say, in the habits of hierarchy begins, in both agrarian and industrial societies, with the patriarchal family. While family structures in which children, women, and servants are treated virtually as chattel have become less authoritarian, the patriarchal family still thrives and could not exactly be called a training ground for autonomy and independence, except perhaps for the male head of household. The patriarchal family historically was rather a training in servitude for most of its members and a training ground of authoritarianism for its male heads of household and its sons-in-training. When the experience of servitude within the family is reinforced by an adult working life lived largely in authoritarian settings that further abridge the workers' autonomy and independence, the consequences for the GHP are melancholy.

The implications of a life lived largely in subservience for the quality of citizenship in a democracy are also ominous. Is it reasonable to expect someone whose waking life is almost completely lived in subservience and who has acquired the habits of survival and self-preservation in such settings to suddenly become, in a town meeting, a courageous, independent-thinking, risk-taking model of individual sovereignty? How does one move directly from what is often a dictatorship at work to the practice of democratic citizenship in the civic sphere? Authoritarian settings do, of course, shape personalities in profound ways. Stanley Milgram famously found that most subjects would administer what they imagined were severe, even life-threatening electric shocks to experimental subjects when directed by authorities in white coats to do so. And Philip Zimbardo found that subjects assigned to role-play prison guards in a psychology experiment were so quick to abuse this power that the experiment had to be aborted before more harm was done.[3]

More generally, political philosophers as varied as Étienne de La Boétie and Jean-Jacques Rousseau were deeply concerned about the political consequences of hierarchy and autocracy. They believed that such settings created the personalities of subjects rather than citizens. Subjects learned the habits of deference. They were apt to fawn on superiors and put on an air of servility, dissembling when necessary and rarely venturing an independent opinion, let alone a controversial one.

Their general demeanor was one of caution. While they may have had views of their own, even subversive ones, they kept such views to themselves, avoiding public acts of independent judgment and moral direction.

Under the most severe forms of "institutionalization" (the term itself is diagnostic), such as prisons, asylums for the mentally ill, orphanages, workhouses for the poor, concentration camps, and old-age homes, there arises a personality disorder sometimes called "institutional neurosis." It is a direct result of long-term institutionalization itself. Those suffering from it are apathetic, take no initiative, display a general loss of interest in their surroundings, make no plans, and lack spontaneity. Because they are cooperative and give no trouble, such institutional subjects may be seen by those in charge in a favorable light, as they adapt well to institutional routines. In the severest cases they may become childish and affect a characteristic posture and gait (in the Nazi concentration camps, such prisoners, near death from privation, were called by other prisoners "*Musselmänner*") and become withdrawn and inaccessible. These are institutional effects produced by the loss of contact with the outside world, the loss of friends and possessions, and the nature of the staff's power over them.

The question I want to pose is this: Are the authoritarian and hierarchical characteristics of most contemporary lifeworld institutions—the family, the school, the factory, the office, the worksite—such that they produce a mild form of institutional neurosis? At one end of an institutional continuum one can place the total institutions that routinely destroy the autonomy and initiative of their subjects. At the other end of this continuum lies, perhaps, some ideal version of Jeffersonian democracy composed of independent, self-reliant, self-respecting, landowning farmers, managers of their own small enterprises, answerable to themselves, free of debt, and more generally with no institutional reason for servility or deference. Such free-standing farmers, Jefferson thought, were the basis of a vigorous and independent public sphere where citizens could speak their mind without fear or favor. Somewhere in between these two poles lies the contemporary situation of most citizens of Western democracies: a relatively open public sphere but a quotidian institutional experience that is largely at cross purposes with the implicit assumptions behind this public sphere and encouraging and often rewarding caution, deference, servility, and conformity. Does this engender a form of institutional neurosis that saps the vitality of civic dialogue? And, more broadly, do the cumulative effects of life within the patriarchal family, the state, and other hierarchical institutions produce a more passive subject who lacks the spontaneous capacity for mutuality so praised by both anarchist and liberal democratic theorists.

If it does, then an urgent task of public policy is to foster institutions that expand the independence, autonomy, and capacities of the citizenry. How is it possible to adjust the institutional lifeworld of citizens so that it is more in keeping with the capacity for democratic citizenship?

FRAGMENT 16
A Modest, Counterintuitive Example: Red
Light Removal

The regulation of daily life is so ubiquitous and so embedded in our routines and expectations as to pass virtually unnoticed. Take the example of traffic lights at intersections. Invented in the United States after World War I, the traffic light substituted the judgment of the traffic engineer for the mutual give-and-take that had prevailed historically between pedestrians, carts, motor vehicles, and bicycles. Its purpose was to prevent accidents by imposing an engineered scheme of coordination. More than occasionally, the result has been the scene in Neubrandenburg with which I opened the book: scores of people waiting patiently for the light to change when it was perfectly apparent there was no traffic whatever. They were suspending their independent judgment out of habit, or perhaps out of a civic fear of the ultimate consequences of exercising it against the prevailing electronic legal order.

What would happen if there were no electronic order at the intersection, and motorists and pedestrians had to exercise their independent judgment? Since 1999, beginning in the city of Drachten, the Netherlands, this supposition has been put to the test with stunning results, leading to a wave of "red light removal" schemes across Europe and in the United States.[4] Both the reasoning behind this small policy initiative and its results are, I believe, diagnostic for other, more far-reaching efforts to craft institutions that enlarge the scope for independent judgment and expand capacities.

Hans Moderman, the counterintuitive traffic engineer who first suggested the removal of a red light in Drachten in 2003, went on to promote the concept of "shared space," which took hold quickly in Europe. He began with the observation that, when an electrical failure incapacitated traffic lights, the result was improved flow rather than congestion. As an experiment, he replaced the busiest traffic-light intersection in Drachten, handling 22,000 cars a day, with a traffic circle, an extended cycle path, and a pedestrian area. In the two years following the removal of the traffic light, the number of accidents plummeted to only two, compared with thirty-six crashes in the four years prior. Traffic moves more briskly through the inter-section when all drivers know they must be alert and use their common sense, while backups and the road rage associated with them have virtually disappeared. Monderman likened it to skaters in a crowded ice rink who manage successfully to tailor their movements to those of the other skaters. He also believed that an excess of signage led drivers to take their eyes off the road, and actually contributed to making junctions less safe.

Red light removal can, I believe, be seen as a modest training exercise in responsible driving and civic courtesy. Monderman was not against traffic lights in principle, he simply did not find any in Drachten that were truly useful in terms of safety, improving traffic flow, and lessening pollution. The traffic circle seems dangerous: and that is the point. He argued that when "motorists are made more wary about how they drive, they behave more carefully," and the statistics on "post–traffic light" accidents bear him out. Having to share the road with other users, and having no imperative coordination imposed by traffic lights, the context virtually requires alertness —an alertness abetted by the law, which, in the case of an accident where blame is hard to determine, presumptively blames the "strongest" (i.e., blames the car driver rather than the bicyclist, and the bicyclist rather than the pedestrian.)

The shared space concept of traffic management relies on the intelligence, good sense, and attentive observation of driv-ers, bicyclists, and pedestrians. At the same time, it arguably, in its small way, actually expands the skills and capacity of drivers, cyclists, and pedestrians to negotiate traffic without being treated like automata by thickets of imperative signs (Germany alone has 648 valid traffic symbols, which accu-mulate as one approaches a town) and signals. Monderman believed that the more numerous the prescriptions, the more it impelled drivers to seek the maximum advantage within the rules: speeding up between signals, beating the light, avoiding all unprescribed courtesies. Drivers had learned to run the maze of prescriptions to their maximum advantage. Without going overboard about its world-shaking significance, Moderman's innovation does make a palpable contribution to the gross human product.

The effect of what was a paradigm shift in traffic management was euphoria. Small towns in the Netherlands put up one sign boasting that they were "Free of Traffic Signs" (*Verkeersbordvrij*), and a conference discussing the new philosophy proclaimed "Unsafe is safe."

FOUR

Two Cheers for the Petty Bourgeoisie

FRAGMENT 17
Introducing a Maligned Class

No increase in material wealth will compensate . . .
for arrangements which insult their self-respect
and impair their freedom.
R. H. Tawney[1]

It is time someone put in a good word for the petite bourgeoisie. Unlike the working class and capitalists, who have
never lack for spokespersons, the petite bourgeoisie rarely, if
ever, speaks for itself. And while capitalists gather in industrial
associations and at the Davos World Economic Forum, and
the working class congregates at trade union congresses, the
one and only time, as near as I can tell, the petite bourgeoisie
gathered in its own name was at the 1901 First International
Congress of the Petite Bourgeoisie in Brussels. There was no
Second Congress.

Why take up the cudgels for a class that remains relatively anonymous and is surely not, in the Marxist parlance, a class *für sich*? There are several reasons. First and most important, I believe that the petite bourgeoisie and small property in general represent a precious zone of autonomy and freedom in state systems increasingly dominated by large public and private bureaucracies. Autonomy and freedom are, along with mutuality, at the center of an anarchist sensibility. Second, I am convinced that the petite bourgeoisie performs vital social and economic services under *any* political system.

Finally, given any reasonably generous definition of its class boundaries, the petite bourgeoisie represents the largest class in the world. If we include not only the iconic shopkeepers but also smallholding peasants, artisans, peddlers, small independent professionals, and small traders whose only property might be a pushcart or a rowboat and a few tools, the class balloons. If we include the periphery of the class, say, tenant farmers, ploughmen with a draft animal, rag pickers, and itinerant market women, where autonomy is more severely constrained and the property small indeed, the class grows even larger. What they all have in common, however, and what distinguishes them from both the clerk and the factory worker is that they are largely in control of their working day and work with little or no supervision. One may legitimately view this as a very dubious autonomy when it means, as a practical matter, working eighteen hours a day for a remuneration that may only provide a bare subsistence. And yet it is clear, as we shall see, that the desire for autonomy, for control over the working day and the sense of freedom and self-respect such control provides, is a vastly underestimated social aspiration for much of the world's population.

FRAGMENT 18
The Etiology of Contempt

Before we start heaping praise on the petite bourgeoisie, we might well pause to consider why it has, as a class, such a bad press. The Marxist contempt for the petite bourgeoisie is in part structural. Capitalist industry created the proletariat, and therefore it is only the proletariat whose emancipation entails the transcending of capitalism as a system. Curiously, but logically, Marxists have a grudging admiration for capitalists who transcended feudalism and unleashed the enormous productive forces of modern industry. They set the stage, as it were, for the proletarian revolution and the triumph of communism amid material plenty. The petite bourgeoisie, by contrast, are neither fish nor fowl; they are mostly poor but they are poor *capitalists*. They may, from time to time, ally with the Left, but they are fair-weather friends; their allegiance is fundamentally unreliable as they have a foot in both camps and desire themselves to become large capitalists.

The direct translation of the French "petite" into English as "petty" rather than, say, "small" does further damage. Now it seems not just to mean small but also contemptibly trivial, as in "pettifoggery," "petty cash," and just plain "petty." And when it is compounded into "petty-bourgeoisie," it joins the contempt of Marxists, the intelligentsia, and the aristocracy for the philistine tastes and crass concern for money and property of the nouveau arrivé. After the Bolshevik Revolution a petty bourgeoisie label could mean prison, exile, or death. The contempt for the petty bourgeoisie was joined to the germ theory of disease in terms foreshadowing Nazi anti-Semitism. Bukharin, stigmatizing the striking workers and sailors, at Kronstadt noted that "the petty bourgeois *infection* had spread from the peasantry to a segment of the working class."[2] Those small peasants who resisted collectivization were castigated in similar terms: "the real danger of bourgeois miasma and petty bourgeois *bacilli* still remains—*disinfection* is necessary."[3] In this last case, the bacilli in question were almost entirely small-holding farmers with a modest surplus who might, at harvest, hire a few laborers. And, of course, the vast majority of the petty bourgeoisie are relatively poor, hardworking, and own barely enough property to make ends meet; the exploitation they practice is largely confined to the patriarchal family— what one writer has termed "auto-exploitation."[4]

The distaste for the petty bourgeoisie also has, I believe, a structural source: one that is shared by the erstwhile social-ist bloc and large capitalist democracies. The fact is, almost all forms of small property have the means to elude the state's control: small property is hard to monitor, tax, or police; it resists regulation and enforcement by the very complexity, va-riety, and mobility of its activities. The crisis of 1929 that led to Stalin's headlong campaign to collectivize was precisely the failure to appropriate sufficient grain from the smallholding peasantry. As a general rule, states of virtually all descriptions have always favored units of production from which it is easier to appropriate grain and taxes. For this reason, the state has nearly always been the implacable enemy of mobile peoples— Gypsies, pastoralists, itinerant traders, shifting cultivators, migrating laborers—as their activities are opaque and mobile, flying below the state's radar. For much the same reason states have preferred agribusiness, collective farms, plantations, and state marketing boards over smallholder agriculture and petty trade. They have preferred large corporations, banks, and business conglomerates to smaller-scale trade and industry. The former are often less efficient than the latter, but the fiscal authorities can more easily monitor, regulate, and tax them. The more pervasive the state's fiscal grasp, the more likely that a "gray" or "black" informal and unreported economy will arise to evade it. And it goes without saying that the sheer size and deep pockets of the largest institutions guarantee them a privileged seat in the councils of power.

FRAGMENT 19
Petty Bourgeois Dreams: The Lure of Property

To make a very long story very short, *Homo sapiens* has been around for something like 200,000 years. States were only "invented" roughly five thousand years ago, and until about a thousand years ago most of humankind lived outside anything that could be called a state. Most of those who did live within those states were small property owners (peasants, artisans, shopkeepers, traders). And, when certain rights of representation developed from the seventeenth century on, they were accorded on the basis of status and property. The large bureaucratic organizations that characterize the modern era may be originally modeled on the monastery and the barracks, but they are essentially a product of the last two and a half centuries. This is another way of saying that there is a long history of life outside the state and that life inside the state until the eighteenth century sharply distinguished between a formally unfree population (slaves, serfs, and dependents), on the one hand, and a large smallholder population on the other that disposed, in theory and often in practice, of certain rights to found families: to hold and inherit land, to form trade associations, to choose local village leaders, and to petition rulers. Relative autonomy and independence for subordinate classes thus came in two forms: a life on the margins, outside the state's reach, or a life inside the state with the minimal rights associated with small property.

I suspect that the tremendous desire one can find in many societies for a piece of land, one's own house, one's own shop owes a great deal not only to the real margin of independent action, autonomy, and security it confers but also to the dignity, standing, and honor associated with small property in the eyes of the state and of one's neighbors. For Thomas Jefferson, independent, smallholding cultivation promoted social virtues and was the bedrock of a democratic citizenry:

> Cultivators of the earth are the most valuable citizens, they are the most vigorous, the most independent, the most virtuous, and they are tied to their country and wedded to its liberty of interest by the most lasting bonds.[5]

In the course of living in and reading about peasant societies, I found it impossible to ignore the incredible tenacity with which many marginal smallholders clung to the smallest patch of land. When pure economic logic suggested they would be far better off seeking a profitable tenancy or even moving to town, they held on by their fingernails as long as they possibly could. Those who had no land of their own to farm sought long-lease tenancies, preferably from relatives, that represented the next best thing, in terms of status, to owning one's own fields. Those who had neither their own land nor a viable tenancy and who were reduced to working for others hung on to their house lot in the village to the bitter end. In terms of sheer income, a good many tenant farmers were better off than smallholders, and a good many laborers were better off than small tenants. For the peasantry, however, the difference in autonomy, independence, and hence social standing was decisive. The smallholder, unlike the tenant, depended on no one for land to farm and the tenant, and unlike the laborer, had at least land for the season and control over his or her working day, while the laborer was cast into what was viewed as a demeaning dependence on the good will of neighbors and relatives. The final humiliation was to lose that last physical symbol of independence, the house lot.

Each of the descending rungs of the village class system represented a loss of economic security and independent status. The substance of the petty bourgeois dream, however, was not some abstract calculation of income security but rather the deep desire for full cultural citizenship in their small community. What property meant was the ability to celebrate marriages, funerals, and, in a small Malay village, the feast at the end of Ramadan, in a way that gave social expression to their worth and standing. The secure "middle peasants" with the steady wherewithal to celebrate these rituals were not only the most influential villagers but also the models to emulate and aspire to. Falling far short of this standard was to become a second-class cultural citizen.

Thwarted petty bourgeois dreams are the standard tinder of revolutionary ferment. "Land to the tiller," in one form or another, has been the effective rallying cry of most agrarian revolutions. The rural revolution in Russia in 1917 was accelerated by the rush of Russian conscripts, defeated on the Austrian front, to return home and participate in the land seizures taking place. For many of the so-called "bare sticks" (unattached, "surplus"), landless laborers in prerevolutionary China, the People's Revolutionary Army represented the precious chance to have land of their own, found a (patriarchal) family, and achieve a passionately desired cultural citizenship that, among other things, meant an honorable burial. The key (bait?) to the enthusiastic participation of the peasantry in virtually all twentieth-century revolutions has been the prospect of land ownership and the standing and independence that came with it. When land reform was succeeded by collectivization, it was experienced and resisted by most of the peasantry as a betrayal of their aspirations.

Petty bourgeois dreams infuse the imagination of the industrial proletariat as well. The reddest of the red proletarians, the militant coal miners and steelworkers of the Ruhr in 1919, on whom Lenin reposed his revolutionary hopes, are a striking case in point.[6] When asked what they wished for, their desires were remarkably modest. They wanted higher wages, a shorter day, and longer rests, as one might expect. But beyond what Marxists would disparagingly call "trade-union consciousness," they yearned to be treated honorably by their bosses (and be called "Herr X") and aspired to have a small cottage with a garden to call their own. It is hardly surprising that a newly industrialized proletariat would retain social aspirations from their village origins, but their demand for the amenities of social respect and for the cultural trappings of an independent life on the land ill fit either the stereotype of an "economistic" working class with both eyes fixed on the loot or that of a revolutionary proletariat.

Over the past several decades, standard opinion polls in the United States have asked industrial workers what kind of work they would prefer to factory work.[7] An astonishingly high percentage pines to open a shop or a restaurant or to farm. The unifying theme of these dreams is the freedom from close supervision and autonomy of the working day that, in their mind, more than compensates for the long hours and risks of such small businesses. Most, of course, never act on this wish, but its tenacity as a fantasy is indicative of its power.

For those who have known real slavery as opposed to "wage slavery," the possibility of an independent subsistence, however marginal, was a dream come true.[8] Slaves throughout the Confederate states, once emancipated, took to their heels and settled on the frontiers of plantation agriculture, making a bare independent livelihood off the unclaimed commons. With a shotgun, a mule, a cow, a fishhook, a few chickens, geese, and a plow, it was finally possible to live independently and to work rarely for "the man," and then only so long as to satisfy the temporary need for cash. Poor whites lived from the commons in much the same way, avoiding a degrading dependence on their wealthier neighbors. The result was the end of the plantation economy, which was only restored, in greatly modified form, with the enactment of the "fence laws" throughout the South from the 1880s on and explicitly designed to close the commons to independent blacks and whites and drive them back into the labor market. The notorious share-cropping system, the closest thing the United States has ever had to serfdom, was the result.

The desire for autonomy seems so powerful that it can take quite perverse forms. In factory settings, where the assembly line is fine-tuned to reduce autonomy to the vanishing point, workers manage nonetheless to steal back autonomous time for "horseplay" as an expression of independence.[9] Auto workers on the line at River Rouge rush to get ahead so they can find a corner to doze in or read or to play a dangerous game of rivet hockey. Workers in socialist Hungary stole time to make "homers"—small lathe pieces for themselves—

even when they had no earthly use for them. In a system of work devised to exterminate "play," the workers refuse this objectification and boredom, asserting their autonomy in creative ways.

Modern agribusiness has, almost diabolically, managed to exploit the desire for small property and autonomy to its own advantage. The practice of contract farming in poultry-raising is a diagnostic example.[10] Knowing that huge confinement operations are epidemiologically dangerous, the largest firms subcontract the raising of fryers to "independent" farmers. The subcontractor is solely responsible for building the large shed required according to the detailed specifications laid down by Tyson or other agribusiness corporations and is responsible for the mortgage needed to finance it. The agribusiness delivers the young chicks and minutely specifies in the contract the feeding, watering, medication, and cleaning regimen, for which it sells the necessary supplies. A subcontractor's daily performance is then closely monitored, and he or she is paid at the end of the contract according to the animals' weight gain and survival rate, with payment calibrated to shifting market conditions. Often the contract will be renewed repeatedly, but there is no guarantee that it will be.

What is perverse about this system is that it preserves a simulacrum of independence and autonomy while emptying out virtually all of its substantive content. The subcontractor is an independent landowner (and mortgage owner), but his workday and movements are nearly as choreographed as those of the assembly-line worker. There is no one immediately breathing down his neck, but if the contract is not renewed, he is stuck with a mortgage as large as his shed. The agribusiness in effect transfers the risks of landownership, of capital on credit, and of managing a large workforce—a workforce that would demand benefits—while reaping most of the advantages of close supervision, standardization, and quality control that the modern factory was originally designed to achieve. And it works! The desire to hold on to the last shred of dignity as an independent property owner is so powerful that the "farmer" is willing to forfeit most of its meaning.

Whatever else they may have missed about the human condition, the anarchists' belief in the drive for the dignity and autonomy of small property was a perceptive reading of the popular imaginary. The petty bourgeois dream of independence, though less attainable in practice, did not die with the Industrial Revolution. Rather, it gained a new lease on life.[11]

FRAGMENT 20
The Not So Petty Social Functions of the Petty Bourgeoisie

From the Diggers and the Levellers of the English Civil War to the Mexican peasants of 1911, to the anarchists of Spain for nearly a century, to a great many anticolonial movements, to mass movements in contemporary Brazil, the desire for land and the restoration of lost land has been the leitmotif of most radically egalitarian mass movements. Without appealing to petty bourgeois dreams, they wouldn't have had a chance.

Marx's contempt for the petite bourgeoisie, second only to his contempt for the *Lumpenproletariat*, was based on the fact that they were small property holders and therefore petty capitalists. Only the proletariat, a new class brought into being by capitalism and without property, could be truly revolutionary; their liberation depended on transcending capitalism. However sound this reasoning in theory, the historical fact is that in the West right up until the end of the nineteenth century, artisans—weavers, shoemakers, printers, masons, cart makers, carpenters—formed the core of most radical working-class movements. As an old class, they shared a communitarian tradition, a set of egalitarian practices, and a local cohesiveness that the newly assembled factory labor force was hard put to match. And, of course, the massive changes in the economy from the 1830s onward threatened their very existence as communities and as trades; they were fighting a rear-guard action to preserve their autonomy. As Barrington Moore, echoing E. P. Thompson, put it,

> the chief social basis of radicalism has been the peasants and the smaller artisans in the towns. From these facts one may conclude that the wellsprings of human freedom lie not only where Marx saw them, in the aspirations of classes about to take power, but perhaps even more in the dying wail of classes over whom the wave of progress is about to roll.[12]

Throughout the Cold War, the standard counterrevolutionary option was preemptive land reform, though it was as often as not blocked by elites. Only after the collapse of the socialist bloc in 1989 did the neoliberal consensus in organizations like the World Bank delete land reform from their policy agenda. While it is also true that beleaguered small property has given rise to more than one right-wing movement, it would be impossible to write the history of struggles for equality without artisans, small peasants, and their passion for the independence of small property near the center of attention.[13]

There is also a strong case to be made for the indispensable economic role of the petty bourgeoisie in invention and innovation. They are the pioneers, if not usually the ultimate beneficiaries, of the great majority of new processes, machines, tools, products, foods, and ideas. Nowhere is this more evident than in the modern software industry, where virtually all the novel ideas have been created by individuals or small partnerships and then purchased or absorbed by larger firms. The role of larger firms has essentially become one of "scouting" the terrain of innovation and then appropriating, by employing, poaching, or buying out, any potentially promising (or threatening) idea. The competitive advantage of large firms lies largely in their capitalization, marketing muscle, lobbying power, and vertical integration, not in their original ideas and innovation. And while it is true that the petty bourgeoisie cannot send a man to the moon, build an airplane, drill for oil in deep water, run a hospital, or manufacture and market a major drug or a mobile phone, the capacity of huge firms to do such things rests substantially on their ability to combine thousands of smaller inventions and processes that they themselves did not and perhaps cannot create.[14] This, too, of course, is an important innovation in its own right. Nevertheless, one key to the oligopoly position of the largest firms lies precisely in their power to eliminate or swallow potential rivals. In doing so, they undoubtedly stifle at least as much innovation as they facilitate.

FRAGMENT 21
"Free Lunches" Courtesy of the Petty Bourgeoisie

If you can't smile, don't open a shop.
Chinese proverb

Not long ago I spent a few days with a friend in Munich at the home of her aging parents whom she had gone to visit. They were relatively frail and largely confined to their apartment, but insistent on walking briefly in the cool summer mornings in their immediate neighborhood. For several days my friend and I accompanied them on their morning shopping rounds, and "rounds" they were. They went first to a small grocery, where they bought a handful of vegetables and some nonperishables; then they proceeded to a nearby shop that carried butter, milk, eggs, and cheese; then to a butcher for a small pork loin; then to a stall selling fruit; and finally, after pausing to watch children playing in a small park, to a newspaper stand for a magazine and the local paper. It seemed a nearly invariant routine, and at each shop there was always a conversation, brief or extended, depending on the number of other shoppers. There were comments on the weather or on a recent traffic accident nearby, inquiries after mutual friends and relatives, mentions of births in the neighborhood, questions on how a son or daughter was getting on, reflections on the annoying traffic noise, and so on.

One could say the conversations were shallow and filled with little more than pleasantries, the small change of daily life, but they were *never* anonymous; the discussants knew one another's name and a fair amount of each other's family history. I was forcibly struck by the easy if thin sociability that prevailed and came to realize that these rounds were the social highlight of my friend's parents' day. They could easily have done most of their shopping more efficiently at a larger store no farther away. On a moment's reflection, one sees that the shopkeepers are unpaid social workers, providing brief but amiable companionship to their steady clientele. "Unpaid" is, of course, not quite right, inasmuch as their prices were surely higher than at the larger outlets; the shopkeepers understood implicitly that the smiles and pleasantries they offered were one way in which they built up a steady and loyal clientele and hence their business. Lest we become overly cynical about the mask of shopkeeper smiles, however, it is worth noting that such pleasantries may well also take the hard edge off a day otherwise spent behind a counter cutting, weighing, and counting money.

The petty bourgeoisie in this small setting perform a kind of daily and reliable social service free of charge that would be hard for a public official or agency to replicate. It is merely one of many gratuitous services the small shopkeepers find it in their own interest to provide in the course of doing business. Jane Jacobs in her deep ethnographic insights into the texture of neighborhoods and public safety has catalogued many of them.[15] Her phrase "eyes on the street," a wholly original observation in 1960, has become a contemporary design principle for urban neighborhoods. It refers to the constant informal monitoring of a neighborhood by pedestrians, shopkeepers, and residents, many of whom are acquainted with one another. Their presence, the animation of the street scene, works to informally preserve public order, with little or no need for intervention. The point for our purposes is that "eyes on the street" requires a dense, mixed-use neighborhood, with many small shops, ateliers, apartments, and services that ensure the steady foot traffic of people on errands, window-shopping, or making deliveries. The anchors of this process are the petty bourgeoisie shopkeepers, who are there most of the day, who know their clients, and who keep an informal eye on the street. Such neighborhoods are far safer than more deserted locales with little foot traffic. Here again a valuable service, in this case ensuring public safety, is provided as a by-product of a combination of other activities and at no cost to the public. Where such informal structures are absent, even the police will find it difficult to maintain effective safety.

The petty bourgeoisie provided services, like the smile of the shopkeeper, that simply cannot be purchased. Jacobs noticed that on virtually every block there was at least one shopkeeper with long hours whom residents asked to hold their apartment keys for out-of-town relatives and friends who would be using their apartment briefly while they were away. The shopkeeper provided this service when asked as a courtesy to his customers. It is impossible to imagine a service like this being provided by a public agency.

It is surely the case that "big box" stores can, owing again to their clout as buyers, deliver a host of manufactured goods to consumers at a cheaper price than the petty bourgeoisie. What is not so clear, however, is whether, once one has factored in all the public goods (the positive externalities) the petty bourgeoisie provides—informal social work, public safety, the aesthetic pleasures of an animated and interesting streetscape, a large variety of social experiences and personalized services, acquaintance networks, informal neighborhood news and gossip, a building block of social solidarity and public action, and (in the case of the smallholding peasantry) good stewardship of the land—the petty bourgeoisie might not be, in a full accounting, a far better bargain, in the long run, than the large, impersonal capitalist firm. And, although they might not quite measure up to the Jeffersonian democratic ideal of the self-confident, independent, land-owning yeoman farmer, they approach it far more closely that the clerk at Wal-Mart or Home Depot.

One final fact is worth noting. A society dominated by smallholders and shopkeepers comes closer to equality and to popular ownership of the means of production than any economic system yet devised.

FIVE

For Politics

FRAGMENT 22
Debate and Quality: Against Quantitative Measures of Qualities

Louisa had been overheard to begin a conversation with her brother one day, by saying, "Tom, I wonder," —upon which Mr. Gradgrind, who was the person overhearing, stepped into the light and said, "Louisa, never wonder."
Herein lay the spring of the mechanical art and mystery of educating the reason, without stooping to the cultivation of the sentiments and affections. Never wonder. By means of addition, subtraction, multiplication, and division, settle everything somehow, and never wonder.

Charles Dickens, Hard Times

The strength of private enterprise lies in its terrifying simplicity . . . it fits perfectly into the modern trend towards total quantification at the expense of the appreciation of qualitative differences; for private enterprise is not concerned with what it produces but with what it gains from production.

E. F. Schumacher, Small Is Beautiful

Mia Kang stared at the test sheet on her desk.

It only was practice. Teachers call it a "field test" to give them an idea of how students will perform on the Texas Assessment of Knowledge and Skills.

But instead of filling in the bubbles and making her teacher happy, Mia, a freshman at MacArthur High School, used her answer sheet to write an essay that challenged standardized testing and using test scores to judge children and rank schools.

"I wrote about how standardized tests are hurting and not helping schools and kids," said Mia, who looks and acts older than her fourteen years. "I just couldn't participate in something that I'm completely opposed to."

"These tests don't measure what kids really need to know, they measure what's easy to measure," she said. "We should be learning concepts and skills, not just memorizing. It's sad for kids and it's sad for teachers, too."

When the teaching and testing implications of No Child Left Behind Act of 2001 finally reached the classroom, there was a flurry of student resistance, of which Mia Kang's brave stand was only a small example. Fifty-eight students at Danvers High School in Massachusetts signed a petition against being required to take the Massachusetts Comprehensive Assessment System (MCAS) exam, and those who refused to sit for the test were suspended from school. Students at other high schools in the state joined them. What might be called "elements of refusal" popped up throughout the country: large numbers of Michigan students opted out of the Michigan Educational Assessment Test, and Wisconsin's high school "exit exam" (a condition of graduation) was scrapped owing to massive resistance from parents and students. In one case, teachers who resented the test drills now required of them protested by collectively refusing their own bonuses for superior performance. Protests against the tests required of early elementary pupils were organized on the pupils' behalf by parents. While understanding the need to guarantee that children became literate and numerate early in their schooling, the parents objected to the "drill and kill" atmosphere in the classroom, as did their children.

A great deal, though not all, of the resistance was provoked by students who hated the "teaching to the test" drills that greatly raised the never negligible quotient of boredom in the classroom to new levels. The test preparation was not merely alienated labor for students and teachers alike, it crowded out the much of the time available for anything else—the arts, drama, history, sports, foreign languages, creative writing, poetry, field trips. Gone were many of the other goals that might animate education: cooperative learning, a multicultural curriculum, the fostering of multiple intelligences, discovery-oriented science, and problem-based learning.

The school was in danger of being transformed into a "one-product" factory, the product being students who could pass standardized tests designed to measure a narrow bandwidth of knowledge and test-taking skills. Here it is worth recalling once again that the modern institution of the school was invented at about the same time as the early textile factory. Each concentrated the workforce under one roof; each created time discipline and task specialization so as to facilitate supervision and evaluation; each aimed at producing a reliable, standardized product. The contemporary emphasis on regional or national standardized tests is based on the model of corporate management by quantitative norms, norms that allow comparisons across teachers, across schools, and across students so as to differentially reward them on the basis of their performance according to this criterion.

The question of the validity of the tests—whether they measure what they purport to measure—is in great doubt. That students can be trained to perform better by drills and by cramming makes it unclear what underlying knowledge or skills the tests measure. They have been shown to consistently underpredict the subsequent performance of women, of African Americans, and of pupils whose first language is not English. Above all, the alienation that high-stakes, test-driven education encourages threatens to give millions of youngsters a lifelong vaccination against school learning altogether.

Those most seemingly in favor of standardized tests as a management tool and a comparative measure of productivity are those at the greatest distance from ground zero of the classroom: superintendents of schools, city and state education officials, governors, and Department of Education policy makers. It gives them all an index, however invalid, of comparative productivity and a powerful incentive system to impose their pedagogical plans. It is most curious that the United States should elect to homogenize its educational system when most of the rest of the world is headed in the opposite direction. Finland, for example, has no external tests and no ranking of students or schools, but scores exceptionally well on all international measures of achievement. Many high-quality colleges and universities have stopped requiring or even encouraging students to take the nationally administered Scholastic Achievement Test (previously the Scholastic *Aptitude* Test).

Nations that have historically relied on a single national examination to allocate precious places in universities have been rushing headlong to eliminate or deemphasize the tests in order to foster "creativity," often in what they take to be an imitation of the American system!

Knowing that their fates and that of their schools depended on test scores each year, many educators not only drilled their students mercilessly but also cheated to ensure a successful outcome. Throughout the nation there was a nationwide epidemic of falsifying results. One of the most recent exposures was in Atlanta, Georgia, where forty-four of fifty-six schools investigated were found to have systematically forged student answers by erasing wrong answers and substituting the correct ones.[1] The Superintendent of Schools, named National Superintendent of the Year in 2009 for her exceptional achievement in raising scores, was found to have created a climate of fear by giving teachers three years to meet targets or be fired. More than 180 educators were implicated in fixing the scores. Like the "brightest people in the room" at Enron, who always found a way to beat the quarterly targets and collect their bonuses, the educators in Atlanta found a way to meet their targets as well, but not in the way anticipated. The stakes were lower, but the collateral damage was equally devastating, and the logic of "gaming the system" was basically the same.

FRAGMENT 23
What If . . . ? An Audit Society Fantasy

Would you please join me in a brief fantasy? The year is 2020. Richard Levin, president of Yale University, has just retired after a long and brilliant tenure and has declared "2020 The

Year of Perfect Vision." Every last building is rebuilt and shining, the students are even more precocious, accomplished, and unionized than they were in 2010, *US News & World Report* and *Consumer Reports* (now merged) have ranked Yale University number 1 across the board—up there with the very best hotels, luxury automobiles, and lawnmowers. Well, nearly across the board. It seems that the quality of the faculty, as reflected in the all-important rankings, has slipped. Yale's competitors are shaking their heads at the decline. Those who know how to read between the lines of apparently serene "Yale Corporation" pronouncements can detect a rising but of course still decorous panic.

One sign of concern can be read from the selection of President Levin's successor, Condoleezza Rice, the retired secretary of state, who most recently led a no-nonsense, business-like streamlining of the Ford Foundation. Yes, she is the first woman of color to lead Yale. Of course, four other Ivy League schools have already been headed by women of color. This is not surprising, inasmuch as Yale has always followed the New England farmer's rule: "Never be the first person to try something new, nor the last."

On the other hand, President Rice wasn't chosen for the symbolism; she was chosen for the promise she represented: the promise of leading a thoroughgoing restructuring of the faculty using the most advanced quality management techniques, techniques perfected from their crude beginnings at the Grandes Écoles of Paris in the late nineteenth century; embodied in Robert McNamara's revolution at Ford and later in his work at the Department of Defense in the 1960s, as well as in Margaret Thatcher's managerial revolution in British social policy and higher education in the 1980s; refined by the development of numerical measures of productivity by individuals and units in industrial management; further developed by the World Bank; and brought to near perfection, so far as higher education is concerned, by the Big Ten universities and making their way, belatedly, to the Ivy League.

We know from confidential sources among the members of the Yale Corporation how Dr. Rice captivated them in her job interview. She said she admired the judicious mix of feudalism (in its politics) and capitalism (in its financial management) that Yale had managed to preserve. It suited perfectly the reforms she had devised—as did Yale's long tradition of what has come to be celebrated as "participatory autocracy" in faculty governance.

But it was her comprehensive plan for massively improving the quality of the faculty—or, more accurately, improving its standing in the national rankings—that convinced the corporation that she was the answer to their prayers.

She excoriated Yale's antiquated practices of hiring, promoting, and tenuring faculty. They were, she said, subjective, medieval, unsystematic, capricious, and arbitrary. These customs, jealously guarded by the aging—largely white male—mandarins of the faculty, whose average age now hovered around eighty, were, she claimed, responsible for Yale's loss of ground to the competition. They produced, on the one hand, a driven, insecure junior faculty who had no way of knowing what the criteria of success and promotion were behind the tastes and prejudices of the seniors in their department and, on the other hand, a self-satisfied, unproductive oligarchy of gerontocrats heedless of the long-run interests of the institution.

Her plan, our sources tell us, was beguilingly simple. She proposed using the scientific techniques of quality evaluation employed elsewhere in the academy but implementing them, for the first time, in a truly comprehensive and transparent fashion. The scheme hinged on the citation indices: the Arts and Humanities Citation Index, the Social Science Citation Index, and, the granddaddy of them all, the Science Citation Index. To be sure, these counts of how often one's work was cited by others in the field were already consulted from time to time in promotion reviews, but as President Rice, she proposed making this form of objective evaluation systematic and comprehensive. The citation indices, she stressed, like the machine counting of votes, play no favorites; they are incapable of conscious or unconscious bias; they represent the only impersonal metric for judgments of academic distinction. They would henceforth be the sole criterion for promotion and tenure. If she succeeded in breaking tenure, it would also serve as a basis for automatically dismissing tenured faculty whose sloth and dimness prevented them from achieving annual citation norms (ACN, for short).

In keeping with the neoliberal emphasis on transparency, full public disclosure, and objectivity, President Rice proposes a modern, high-tech, academic version of Robert Owens's factory scheme at New Lanark. The entire faculty is to be outfitted with digitalized beanies. As soon as they are designed—in Yale's distinctive blue-and-white color scheme—and can be manufactured under humane, nonsweatshop conditions, using no child labor, all faculty will be required to wear them on campus. The front of the beanie, across the forehead, will consist in a digital screen, rather like a taxi meter, on which will be displayed the total citation count of that scholar in real time. As the fully automated citation recording centers register new citations, these citations, conveyed by satellite, will be posted automatically to the digital readout on the beanie. Think of a miniature version of the constantly updated world population count once available in lights in Times Square. Let's call it the Public Record of Digitally Underwritten Citation Totals, which produces the useful acronym PRODUCT. Rice conjures a vision of the thrill students will experience as they listen, rapt, to the lecture of a brilliant and renowned professor whose beanie, while she lectures, is constantly humming, the total citations piling up before their very eyes. Meanwhile, in a nearby classroom, students worry as they contemplate the blank readout on the beanie of the embarrassed professor before them. How will their transcript look when the cumulative citation total of all the professors from whom they have taken courses is compared with the cumulative total of their competitors for graduate or professional school? Have they studied with the best and brightest?

Students will no longer have to rely on the fallible hearsay evidence of their friends or the prejudices of a course critique. The numerical "quality grade" of their instructor will be there for all to see and to judge. Junior faculty no longer need fear the caprice of their senior colleagues. A single, indisputable standard of achievement will, like a batting average, provide a measure of quality and an unambiguous target for ambition. For President Rice, the system solves the perennial problem of how to reform departments that languish in the backwaters of their disciplines and become bastions of narrow patronage. This publicly accountable, transparent, impersonal measure of professional standing shall henceforth be used, in place of promotion and hiring committees.

Think of the clarity! A blue-ribbon panel of distinguished faculty (chosen by the new criterion) will simply establish several citation plateaus: one for renewal, one for promotion to term associate, one for tenure, and one for post-tenure performance. After that, the process will be entirely automated once the beanie technology is perfected. Imagine a much-quoted, pace-setting political science professor, Harvey Writealot, lecturing to a packed hall on campus. Suddenly, because an obscure scholar in Arizona has just quoted his last article in the *Journal of Recent Recondite Research* and, by chance, that very citation is the one that puts him over the top, the beanie instantly responds by flashing the good news in blue and white and playing "Boola-Boola." The students, realizing what has happened, rise to applaud their professor's elevation. He bows modestly, pleased and embarrassed by the fuss, and continues the lecture—but now with tenure. The console on the desk of President Rice's office in Woodbridge Hall tells her that Harvey has made it" into the magic circle on his own merits, and she in turn sends him a message of congratulations broadcast through the beanie by text and voice. A new, distinctive "tenure beanie" and certificate will follow shortly.

Members of the corporation, understanding instantly how much time and disputation this automated system could save and how it could catapult Yale back into the faculty ratings chase, set about refining and perfecting the technique. One suggests having a time-lapse system of citation depreciation, each year's citations losing one-eighth of their value with each passing year. An eight-year-old citation would evaporate, in keeping with the pace of field development. Reluctantly, one member of the corporation suggests that, for consistency, there be a minimal plateau for retention, even of previously tenured faculty. She acknowledges that the image of a bent professor's citation total degrading to the dismissal level in the middle of a seminar is a sad spectacle to contemplate. Another suggests that the beanie in such a case could simply be programmed to go completely blank, though one imagines the professor could read his fate in the averted gaze of his students.

My poking fun at quantitative measures of productivity in the academy, however satisfying in its own right, is meant to serve a larger purpose. The point I wish to make is that democracies, particularly mass democracies like the United States that have embraced meritocratic criteria for elite selection and the distribution of public funds, are tempted to develop impersonal, objective, mechanical measures of quality. Regardless of the form they take: the Social Science Citation Index, the Scholastic Aptitude Test (renamed the Scholastic Assessment Test and, more recently, the Scholastic Reasoning Test), cost-benefit analysis—they all follow the same logic. Why? The short answer is that there are few social decisions as momentous for individuals and families as the distribution of life chances through education and employment or as momentous for communities and regions as the distribution of public funds for public works projects. The seductiveness of such measures is that they all turn measures of quality into measures of quantity, thereby allowing comparison across cases with an apparently single and impersonal metric. They are above all a vast and deceptive "antipolitics machine" designed to turn legitimate political questions into neutral, objective administrative exercises governed by experts. It is this depoliticizing sleight-of-hand that masks a deep lack of faith in the possibilities of mutuality and learning in politics so treasured by anarchists and democrats alike. Before arriving at "politics," however, there two other potentially fatal objections to such techniques of quantitative commensuration.

FRAGMENT 24
Invalid and Inevitably Corrupt

The first and most obvious problem with such measures is that they are often invalid; that is, they rarely measure the quality we believe to be at stake with any accuracy.

The Science Citation Index (SCI), founded in 1963 and the granddaddy of all citation indices, was the brainchild of Eugene Garfield. Its purpose was to gauge, to measure the scientific impact of, say, a particular research paper, and by extension a particular scholar or research laboratory, by the frequency with which a published paper was cited by other research scientists. Why not? It sure beat relying on informal reputations, grants, the obscure embedded hierarchies of established institutions, let alone the sheer productivity of a scholar. More than half of all scientific publications, after all, seem to sink without a trace; they aren't cited at all, not even once! Eighty percent are only cited once, ever. The SCI seemed to offer a neutral, accurate, transparent, disinterested, and objective measure of a scholar's impact on subsequent scholarship. A blow for merit! And so it was, at least initially, compared to the structures of privilege and position it claimed to replace.

It was a great success, not least because it was heavily promoted; let's not forget that this is a for-profit business! Soon it was pervasive: used in the award of tenure, to promote journals, to rank scholars and institutions, in technological analyses and government studies. Soon the Social Science Citation Index (SSCI) followed and, after that, could the Arts and Humanities Citation Index be far behind?

What precisely did the SCI measure? The first thing to notice is the computer-like mindlessness and abstraction of the data gathering. Self-citations counted, adding auto-eroticism to the normal narcissism that prevails in the academy. Negative citations, "X's article is the worst piece of research I have ever encountered," also count. Score one for X! As Mae West said, "There's no such thing as bad publicity; just spell my name right!" Citations found in books, as opposed to articles, are not canvassed. More seriously, what if absolutely NO ONE EVER READS the articles in which a work was cited, as is often the case? Then there is the provincialism of the exercise; this is, after all a massively English-language, and hence Anglo-American, operation. Garfield claimed that the provincialism of French science could be seen in is failure to adopt English as *the* language of science. In the social sciences, this is preposterous on its face, but it is true that the translation and sale of your work to a hundred thousand Chinese, Brazilians, or Indonesian intellectuals will add nothing to your SSCI standing unless they record their gratitude in an English-language journal or in one of the handful of foreign language journals included in the magic circle.

Notice, too that the index must, as a statistical matter, favor the specialties that are the most heavily trafficked, that is to say mainstream research or, in Kuhn's terms, "normal science." Notice finally that the "objectified subjectivity" of the SSCI also is supremely presentist. What if a current line of inquiry is dropped as a sterile exercise three years hence? Today's wave, and the statistical blip it creates, may still have allowed our lucky researcher to surf to a safe harbor despite her mistake. There is no need to belabor these shortcomings of the SSCI further. They serve only to show the inevitable gap between measures of this kind and the underlying quality they purport to assess. The sorry fact is, many of these shortcomings could be rectified by reforms and elaborations of the procedures by which the index is constructed. In practice, however, the more schematically abstract and computationally simple measure is preferred for its ease of use and, in this case, lower cost. But beneath the apparently objective metric of citations lies a long series of "accounting conventions" smuggled into measurements that are deeply political and deeply consequential.

My fun at the expense of the SSCI may seem a cheap shot. The argument I'm making, however, applies to *any* quantitative standard rigidly applied. Take the apparently reasonable "two-book" standard often applied in some departments at Yale in tenure decisions. How many scholars are there whose single book or article has generated more intellectual energy than the collected works of other, quantitatively far more "productive," scholars? The commensurating device known as the "tape measure" may tell us that a Vermeer interior and a cow plop are both twenty inches across; there, however, the similarity ends.

The second fatal flaw is that even if the measure, when first devised, was a valid measure, its very existence typically sets in motion a train of events that undermines its validity. Let's call this a process by which "a measure colonizes behavior," thereby negating whatever validity it once had. Thus, I have been told there are "rings" of scholars who have agreed to cite one another routinely and thereby raise their citation rating! Outright conspiracy of this kind is but the most egregious version of a more important phenomenon. Simply knowing that the citation index can make or break a career exerts a not-so-subtle influence on professional conduct: for example, the gravitational pull of mainstream methodologies and populous subfields, the choice of journals, the incantation of a field's most notable figures are all encouraged by the incentives thereby conjured. This is not necessarily crass Machiavellian behavior; I'm pointing instead to the constant pressure at the margin to act "prudently." The result, in the long run, is a selection pressure, in the Darwinian sense, favoring the survival of those who meet or exceed their audit quotas.

A citation index is not merely an observation; it is a force in the world, capable of generating its own observations. Social theorists have been so struck by this colonization that they have attempted to give it a lawlike formulation in Goodhart's law, which holds that "when a measure becomes a target it ceases to be a good measure."[2] And Matthew Light clarifies: "An authority sets some quantitative standard to measure a particular achievement; those responsible for meeting that standard, do so, but not in the way which was intended."

A historical example will clarify what I mean. The officials of the French absolutist kings sought to tax their subjects' houses according to size. They seized on the brilliant device of counting the windows and doors of a dwelling. At the beginning of the exercise, the number of windows and doors was a nearly perfect proxy for the size of a house. Over the next two centuries, however, the "window and door tax," as it was called, impelled people to reconstruct and rebuild houses so as to minimize the number of apertures and thereby reduce the tax. One imagines generations of French choking in their poorly ventilated "tax shelters." What started out as a valid measure became an invalid measure.

But this kind of policy is not limited to windows or pre-revolutionary France. Indeed, similar methods of audit and quality control have come to dominate the educational system throughout much of the world. In the United States, the SAT has come to represent the technique of quantification that serves to distribute higher educational opportunities in an apparently objective fashion. We could just as easily take up the "exam hell" that dominates the gateway to university education, and thereby life chances, in any number of other countries.

Let's just say that with respect to education, the SAT is not just the tail that wags the dog. It has reshaped the dog's breed, its appetite, its surroundings, and the lives of all those who care for it and feed it. It's a striking example of colonization. A set of powerful quantitative observations, once again, create something of a social Heisenberg Principle in which the scramble to make the grade utterly transforms the observational field. "Quantitative technologies work best," Porter reminds us, "if the world they aim to describe can be remade in their own image."[3] It's a fancy way of saying that the SAT has so reshaped education after its monochromatic image that what it observes is largely the effect of what it has itself conjured up.

Thus the desire to measure intellectual quality by standardized tests *and* to use those tests to distribute rewards to students, teachers, and schools has perverse colonizing effects. A veritable multi-million-dollar industry markets cram courses and techniques that purport to improve performance on tests that were said to be immune to such stratagems. Stanley Kaplan's empire of test preparation courses and workbooks was built on the premise that one could learn to beat the test for college, law school, medical school, etc. The all-powerful audit criteria circle back, as it were, and colonize the lifeworld of education; the measurement replaces the quality it is supposed only to assess. There ensues something like an arms race in which the test formulators try to outwit the test preparation salesmen. The measurement ends by corrupting the desired substance or quality. Thus, once the "profile" of a successful applicant to an Ivy League school becomes known, the possibility of gaming the system arises. Education consultants are hired by wealthy parents to advise their children, with one eye on the Ivy League profile, about what extracurricular activities are desirable, what volunteer work might be advantageous, and so on. What began as a good faith exercise to make judgments of quality becomes, as parents try to "position" their children, a strategy. It becomes nearly impossible to assess the meaning or authenticity of such audit-corrupted behavior.

The desire for measures of performance that are quantitative, impersonal, and objective was, of course, integral to the management techniques brought from Ford Motor Company to the Pentagon by "whiz kid" Robert McNamara and applied to the war in Indochina. In a war without clearly demarcated battle lines, how could one gauge progress? McNamara told General Westmoreland, "General, show me a graph that will tell me whether we are winning or losing in Vietnam." The result was at least two graphs: one, the most notorious, was an index of attrition, in which the "body counts" of confirmed enemy personnel killed in action were aggregated. Under enormous pressure to show progress, and knowing that the figures influenced promotions, decorations, and rest-and-recreation decisions, those who did the accounting made sure the body counts swelled. Any ambiguity between civilian and military casualties was elided; virtually all dead bodies became enemy military personnel. Soon, the total of enemy dead exceeded the known combined strength of the so-called Viet Cong and the North Vietnamese forces troop levels. Yet in the field, the enemy was anything but defeated.

The second index was an effort to take the measure of civilian sympathies in the campaign to Win Hearts and Minds—WHAM. The Hamlet Evaluation System was at its core: every one of South Vietnam's 12,000 hamlets was classified according to an elaborate scheme as "pacified," "contested," or "hostile." Pressure to show progress was again unrelenting.

Ways were found: by fudging figures, by creating on paper self-defense militias that would have made Tsarina Catherine's minister Grigory Potemkin proud, by statistically ignoring incidents of insurgent activity, in order to have the graph show improvement. Outright fraud, though not rare, was less common than the understandable tendency to resolve all ambiguities in the direction the incentives for a favorable evaluation and promotion led. Gradually, it seemed, the countryside was being pacified.

McNamara had created an infernal audit system that not only produced a mere simulacrum—a "command performance," as it were—of legible progress but also blocked a wider-ranging dialogue about what might, under these circumstances, represent progress. They might have heeded a real scientist's words, Einstein's: "Not everything that counts can be counted and not everything that can be counted, counts."

Finally, a more recent instance of this dynamic, with which many American investors have become sadly familiar, is furnished by the collapse of Enron Corporation. In the 1960s, business schools were preoccupied with the problem of how to "discipline" corporate managers so that they would not serve their own narrow interests at the expense of the interests of the company's owners (aka shareholders). The solution they devised was to tie the compensation of senior management to business performance, as measured by shareholder value (aka share price). As their compensation in stock options depended, usually quarterly, on the share price, managers quickly responded by devising techniques in collaboration with their accountants and auditors to so cook the books that they would meet their quarterly share-price target and receive their bonuses. To boost the value of the company's stock, they inflated profits and concealed losses so that others would be deceived into bidding up the share price. Thus, the attempt to make executive performance completely transparent by largely replacing salaries, given as a reward for labor and expertise, with stock option plans backfired. A similar "gaming logic" was at work in the bundling of mortgages into complex financial instruments implicated in the world financial collapse of 2008. Bond rating agencies, aside from being paid by bond issuers, had, in the interest of transparency, made their rating formulas available to investment firms. Knowing the procedures, or better yet hiring away the raters themselves, it became possible to reverse-engineer bonds with the formulas in mind and thereby achieve top ratings (AAA) for financial instruments that were exceptionally risky. Once again, the audit was successful but the patient died.

FRAGMENT 25
Democracy, Merit, and the End of Politics

The great appeal of quantitative measures of quality arises, I believe, from two sources: a democratizing belief in equality of opportunity as opposed to inherited privilege, wealth, and entitlement, on the one hand, and a modernist conviction that merit can be scientifically measured on the other.

Applying scientific laws and quantitative measurement to most social problems would, modernists believed, eliminate sterile debates once the "facts" were known. This lens on the world has, built into it, a deeply embedded political agenda. There are, on this account, facts (usually numerical) that require no interpretation. Reliance on such facts should reduce the destructive play of narratives, sentiment, prejudices, habits, hyperbole, and emotion generally in public life. A cool, clinical, quantitative assessment would resolve disputes. Both the passions and the interests would be replaced by neutral, technical judgment. These scientific modernists aspired to minimize the distortions of subjectivity and partisan politics to achieve what Lorraine Daston has called "a-perspectival objectivity," a view from nowhere.[4] The political order most compatible with this view was the disinterested, impersonal rule of a technically educated elite using its scientific knowledge to regulate human affairs. This aspiration was seen as a new "civilizing project." The reformist, cerebral Progressives in early twentieth-century American and, oddly enough, Lenin as well believed that objective scientific knowledge would allow the "administration of things" to largely replace politics. Their gospel of efficiency, technical training, and engineering solutions implied a world directed by a trained, rational, and professional managerial elite.

The idea of a meritocracy is the natural traveling companion of democracy and scientific modernism.[5] No longer would a ruling class be an accident of noble birth, inherited wealth, or inherited status of any kind. Rulers would be selected, and hence legitimated, by virtue of their skills, intelligence, and demonstrated knowledge. (Here I pause to observe how other qualities one might plausibly want in positions of power, such as compassion, wisdom, courage, or breadth of experience, drop out of this account entirely.) Intelligence, by the standards of the time, was assumed by most of the educated public to be a measurable quality. Most assumed, furthermore, that intelligence was distributed, if not randomly, then at least far more widely than either wealth or title. The very idea of distributing, for the first time, position and life chances on the basis of measurable merit was a breath of democratic fresh air. It promised for society as a whole what Napoleon's merit-based "careers open to talent" had promised the new professional middle class in France more than a century earlier.

Notions of a measurable meritocracy were democratic in still another sense: they severely curtailed the claims to discretionary power previously claimed by professional classes. Historically, the professions operated as trade guilds, setting their own standards, jealously guarding their professional secrets, and brooking no external scrutiny that would overrule their judgment. Lawyers, doctors, chartered accountants, engineers, and professors were hired for their professional judgment—a judgment that was often ineffable and opaque.

Fragment 26
In Defense of Politics

> The mistakes made by a revolutionary workers movement are immeasurably more fruitful and more valuable than the infallibility of any party.
> *Rosa Luxemburg*

The real damage of relying mainly on quantitatively measured merit and "objective" numerical audit systems to assess quality arises from taking vital questions that ought to be part of a vigorous democratic debate off the table and placing them in the hands of presumably neutral experts. It is this spurious depoliticization of momentous decisions affecting the life chances of millions of citizens and communities that deprives the public sphere of what legitimately belongs to it. If there is one conviction that anarchist thinkers and nondemagogic populists share, it is a faith in the capacity of a democratic citizenry to learn and grow through engagement in the public sphere. Just as we might ask what kind of person a particular office or factory routine produces, so might we want to ask how a political process might expand citizen knowledge and capacities. In this respect, the anarchist belief in mutuality without hierarchy and the capacity of ordinary citizens to learn through participation would deplore this short-circuiting of democratic debate. We can see the antipolitics machine at work in the uses of the Social Science Citation Index (SSCI), the Scholastic Aptitude Test (SAT), and in the now ubiquitous cost-benefit analysis.

The antipolitics of the SSCI consists in substituting a pseudo-scientific calculation for a healthy debate about quality. The real politics of a discipline—its worthy politics, anyway—is precisely the dialogue about standards of value and knowledge. I entertain few illusions about the typical quality of that dialogue. Are there interests and power relations at play? You bet. They're ubiquitous. There is, however, no substitute for this necessarily qualitative and always-inconclusive discussion. It is the lifeblood of a discipline's character, fought out in reviews, classrooms, roundtables, debates, and decisions about curriculum, hiring, and promotion. Any attempt to curtail that discussion by, for example, Balkanization into quasi-autonomous subfields, rigid quantitative standards, or elaborate scorecards tends simply to freeze a given orthodoxy or division of spoils in place.

The SAT system has, over the past half century, been opening and closing possible futures for millions of students. It has helped fashion an elite. Little wonder that that elite looks favorably on the system that helped it get to the front of the pack. It is just open enough, transparent enough, and impartial enough to allow elites and nonelites to regard it as a fair national competition for advancement. More than wealth or birth ever could, it allows the winners to see their reward as merited, although the correlations between SAT scores and socioeconomic status are enough to convince an impartial observer that this is no open door. The SAT, in effect, selected an elite that is more impartially chosen than its predecessors, more legitimate, and hence better situated to defend and reinforce the institution responsible for the naturalization of their excellence.

In the meantime, our political life is impoverished. The hold of the SAT convinces many middle-class whites that affirmative action is a stark choice between objective merit, on the one hand, and rank favoritism on the other. We are deprived of a public dialogue about how educational opportunity ought to be allocated in a democratic and plural society. We are deprived of a debate about what qualities we might want in our elites, individually in our schools, insofar as curricula simply echo the tunnel vision of the SAT.

An example drawn from a different field of public policy illustrates the way in which debatable assumptions are smuggled into the very structure of most audits and quantitative indices. Cost-benefit analysis, pioneered by the engineers of the French École des Ponts et Chausées and now applied by development agencies, planning bodies, the U.S. Army Corps of Engineers, and the World Bank for virtually all their initiatives, is a striking case in point. Cost-benefit analysis is a series of valuation techniques designed to calculate the rate of return for any given project (a road, a bridge, a dam, a port). This requires that all costs and returns be monetized so that they can be subsumed under the same metric. Thus the cost of, say, the loss of a species of fish, the loss of a beautiful view, of jobs, of clean air, if it is to enter the calculus, must be expressed in dollar terms. This requires some heroic assumptions. For the loss of a beautiful view, "shadow pricing" is used whereby residents are asked how much they would be willing to add to their taxes to preserve the view. The sum then becomes its value! If fishermen sold the fish extinguished by a dam, the loss of sales would represent their value. If they were not sold, then they would be valueless for the purpose of the analysis. Osprey, otters, and mergansers might be disappointed at the loss of their livelihood, but only human losses count. Losses that cannot be monetized cannot enter the analysis. When, say, an Indian tribe refuses compensation and declares that the graves of their ancestors, shortly to be flooded behind a dam, are "priceless beyond measure," it defies the logic of cost-benefit analysis and falls out of the equation.

Everything, all costs and benefits, must be made commensurate and monetized in order to enter the calculations for the rate of return: a sunset view, trout, air quality, jobs, recreation, water quality. Perhaps the most heroic of the assumptions behind cost-benefit analysis is the value of the *future*. The question arises, how is one to calculate future benefits—say, a gradually improving water quality or future job gains? In general, the rule is that future benefits will be *discounted at the current or average rate of interest*. As a practical matter this means that virtually any benefit, unless massive, more than five years in the future will be negligible once discounted in this fashion. Here, then, is a critical political decision about the value of the future that is smuggled into the cost-benefit formula as a mere *accounting convention*. Quite apart from the manipulations to which cost-benefit analysis has always been subject, the great damage it does, even when rigorously applied, is its radical depoliticization of public decision making.

Porter attributes the adoption of audit systems of this kind in the United States to a "lack of trust in bureaucratic elites" and suggests that the United States "relies on rules to control the exercise of official judgment to a greater extent than any other industrialized democracy."[6] Thus, audit systems of this kind with the aim of achieving total objectivity by suppressing all discretion represent both the apotheosis of technocracy and its nemesis.

Each technique is an attempt to substitute a transparent, mechanical, explicit, and usually numerical procedure of evaluation for the suspect and apparently undemocratic practices of a professional elite. Each is a rich paradox from top to bottom, for the technique is also a response to political pressure: the desire of a clamorous public for procedures of decision and, in effect, rationing that are explicit, transparent, and, hence, in principle, accessible. Although cost-benefit analysis is a response to public political pressure—and here is one paradox—its success depends absolutely on appearing totally nonpolitical: objective, nonpartisan, and palpably scientific. Beneath this appearance, of course, cost-benefit analysis is deeply political. Its politics are buried deep in the techniques of calculation: in what to measure in the first place, in how to measure it, in what scale to use, in conventions of "discounting" and "commensuration," in how observations are translated into numerical values, and in how these numerical values are used in decision making. While fending off charges of bias or favoritism, such techniques—and here is a second paradox—succeed brilliantly in entrenching a political agenda at the level of procedures and conventions of calculation that is doubly opaque and inaccessible.

When they are successful politically, the techniques of the SAT, cost-benefit analysis, and, for that matter, the Intelligence Quotient appear as solid, objective, and unquestionable as numbers for blood pressure, thermometer readings, cholesterol levels, and red blood cell counts. The readings are perfectly impersonal and, so far as their interpretation is concerned, "the doctor knows best."

They seem to eliminate the capricious human element in decisions. Indeed, once the techniques with their deeply embedded and highly political assumptions are firmly in place, they *do* limit the discretion of officials. Charged with bias, the official can claim, with some truth, that "I am just cranking the handle"—of a nonpolitical decision-making machine. The vital protective cover such antipolitics machines provide helps explain why their validity is of less concern than their standardization, precision, and impartiality. Even if the SSCI does not measure the quality of a scholar's work, even if the SAT doesn't really measure intelligence or predict success in college, each constitutes an impartial, precise, public standard, a transparent set of rules and targets. When such tools succeed, they achieve the necessary alchemy of taking contentious and high-stakes battles for resources, life chances, mega-project benefits, and status and transmuting them into technical, apolitical decisions presided over by officials whose neutrality is beyond reproach. The criteria for decisions are explicit, standardized, and known in advance. Discretion and politics are made to disappear by techniques that are, at bottom, completely saturated with discretionary choices and political assumptions, now shielded effectively from public view.

The widespread use of numerical indices is not limited to any country, any branch of public policy, or indeed to the immediate present. Its current vogue in the form of the "audit society" obviously owes something to the rise of the large corporation, whose shareholders seek to measure productivity and results, and to the neoliberal politics of the 1970s and 1980s, as exemplified by Thatcher and Reagan, Their emphasis on "value for money" in public administration, borrowing techniques from management science in the private sector, sought to establish scores and "league tables" for schools, hospitals, police and fire departments, and so on. The deeper cause, however, is, paradoxically again, democratization and the demand for political control of administrative decisions. The United States seems to be something of an outlier in its embrace of audits and quantification. No other country has embraced audits in education, war-making, public works, and the compensation of business executives as enthusiastically as has the United States. Contrary to their self-image as a nation of rugged individualists, Americans are among the most normalized and monitored people in the world.

The great flaw of all these administrative techniques is that, in the name of equality and democracy, they function as a vast "antipolitics machine," sweeping vast realms of legitimate public debate out of the public sphere and into the arms of technical, administrative committees. They stand in the way of potentially bracing and instructive debates about social policy, the meaning of intelligence, the selection of elites, the value of equity and diversity, and the purpose of economic growth and development. They are, in short, the means by which technical and administrative elites attempt to convince a skeptical public—while excluding that public from the debate—that they play no favorites, take no obscure discretionary action, and have no biases but are merely making transparent technical calculations. They are, today, the hallmark of a neoliberal political order in which the techniques of neoclassical economics have, in the name of scientific calculation and objectivity, come to replace other forms of reasoning.[7] Whenever you hear someone say "I'm deeply invested in him/her" or refer to social or human "capital" or, so help me, refer to the "opportunity cost" of a human relationship, you'll know what I'm talking about.

SIX

Particularity and Flux

History is written by learned men, and so it is natural and agreeable
for them to think that the activity of their class supplies the basis of
the movement of all humanity.
Leo Tolstoy, War and Peace

FRAGMENT 27
Retail Goodness and Sympathy

The heroism of the French town of Le Chambon-sur-Lignon,
in the Haute-Loire, which managed to shelter, feed, and speed
to safety more than five thousand refugees in Vichy France,
many of them Jewish children, is by now enshrined in the an-
nals of resistance to Nazism. Books and films have celebrated
the many acts of quiet bravery that made this uncommon res-
cue possible.

Here I want to emphasize the *particularity* of these acts in
a way that, though it may diminish the grand narrative of religious resistance to anti-Semitism, at the same time enlarges
our understanding of the specificity of humanitarian gestures.

Many Le Chambon villagers were Huguenot, and their two
pastors were perhaps the most influential and respected voices
in the community. As Huguenots, they had their own collec-

tive memory, from at least the St. Bartholomew's Day Massacre forward, of religious persecution and flight. Well before the Occupation, they had manifested their sympathy for the victims of fascism by sheltering refugees from Franco's Spain and Mussolini's Italy. That is, they were well disposed both by conviction and experience to sympathize with the plight of refugees from authoritarian states, and with Jews in particular as a biblical people. Translating that sympathy into practical and, under Vichy, far more dangerous acts of assistance, however, was not so simple.

Anticipating the arrival of Jews, the Huguenot pastors began trying to mobilize the clandestine shelter and food they knew would be required of their parishioners. With the abolition of the Free Zone in southern France, both pastors were arrested and taken off to concentration camps. In this menacing setting, the wives of the two pastors took up their husbands' work and set about lining up food and shelter for Jews within their community. They asked their neighbors, both farmers and villagers, if they would be willing to help when the time came. The answers often were not encouraging. Typically, those they asked expressed sympathy for the refugees but were unwilling to run the risk of taking them in and feeding them. They pointed out that they also had a duty to protect their own immediate family and were fearful that if they sheltered Jews, they would be denounced to the local Gestapo, who would put them and their entire family at grave risk. Weighing their obligations to their immediate family and their more abstract sympathy for helping Jewish victims, family ties prevailed, and the pastor's wives despaired of organizing a network of refuge.

Whether they were ready or not, however, the Jews began to arrive, and to seek help. What happened next is important, and diagnostic for understanding the particularity of social (in this case, humanitarian) action. The pastors' wives found themselves with real, existing Jews on their hands, and they tried again. They would, for example, take an elderly Jew, thin and shivering in the cold, to the door of a farmer who had declined to commit himself earlier, and ask, "Would you give our friend here a meal and a warm coat, and show him the way to the next village?" The farmer now had a living, breathing victim in front of him, looking him in the eye, perhaps imploringly, and would have to turn him away. Or the women would arrive at the farmhouse door with a small family and ask, "Would you give this family a blanket, a bowl of soup, and let them sleep in your barn for a day or two before they head for the Swiss border?" Face-to-face with real victims, whose fate depended palpably on their assistance, few were willing to refuse them help, though the risks had not changed.

Once the individual villagers had made such a gesture, they typically became committed to helping the refugees for the duration. They were, in other words, able to draw the conclusions of their own practical gesture of solidarity—their actual line of conduct—and see it as the ethical thing to do. They did not enunciate a principle and then act on it. Rather, they acted, and then drew out the logic of that act. Abstract principle was the child of practical action, not its parent.

François Rochat, contrasting this pattern with Hannah Arendt's "banality of evil," calls it "the banality of goodness."[1] We might at least as accurately call it the "particularity of goodness," or, to appropriate the Torah, an example of the heart following the hand.

The particularity of identification and sympathy is a working assumption of journalism, poetry, and charitable work.

People don't easily identify with or open their hearts or wallets for large abstractions: the Unemployed, the Hungry, the Persecuted, the Jews. But portray in gripping detail, with photographs, a woman who has lost her job and is living in her car, or a refugee family on the run through the forest living on roots and tubers, and you are likely to engage the sympathy of strangers. All victims cannot easily represent one victim, but one victim can often stand for a whole class of victims.

This principle was powerfully at work in the most moving memorial for Holocaust victims I have ever seen, an exhibition in the great town hall of Münster, where the Treaty of Westphalia was signed in 1648, ending the Thirty Years' War. Street by street, address by address, name by name, the fate of *each and every* Jewish family (some six thousand of them) was depicted. There was usually a photograph of the house in which the family lived (most still standing, as Münster was largely spared Allied bombing), the street address, sometimes an identity card or a carte de visite, photographs of the family individually and together (at a picnic, a birthday party, a family photo-portrait), and a note as to their fate: "murdered at Bergen-Belsen," "fled to France and then Cuba," "migrated to Israel from Morocco," "fled to Lodz, Poland, fate unknown." In quite a few cases there were no photographs, just a dotted rectangle indicating where a photograph would go.

It was, above all, a *municipal* exhibition for the citizenry of Münster. They could stroll from street to street, as it were, and see the Jews who had been their neighbors or those of their parents and grandparents, their houses, their faces—often reflecting happier moments—beaming out at them. It was the powerful particularity, the individuality, and its massive repetition that made it so memorable in the literal sense of the word.[2] How much more moving it was than many of the other ubiquitous collective memorials to Jews, homosexuals ("On this street corner, homosexuals were assembled for transport to the concentration camps"), handicapped, and Gypsies (Roma and Sinti)![3]

Perhaps the most stunning thing about this exhibition, however, was the very process by which it was created. Hundreds of Münster citizens had worked for more than a decade, combing records, authenticating deaths, tracing survivors, and writing personal letters to the thousands they could track, explaining the exhibition they were preparing and asking if the respondents would be willing to complete the record and to contribute a photograph or a note. Many, understandably, refused; many others sent something, and a good many came to Münster to see for themselves. The result spoke for itself, but the process of tracing family histories, locating survivors and their children, and writing them personal letters as star-crossed neighbors across the void of history and death itself was a cathartic, if not cleansing, recognition of a shared and tragic history. Most of those preparing the exhibition were not even born when the Jews were scourged, and one imagines the thousands of painful conversations and recollections the process touched off among the generations in Münster.

FRAGMENT 28
Bringing Particularity, Flux, and
Contingency Back In

The job of most history and social science is to summarize, codify, and otherwise "package" important social movements and major historical events, to make them legible and understandable. Given this objective and the fact that the events they are seeking to illuminate have already happened, it is hardly surprising that historians and social scientists should typically give short shrift to the confusion, flux, and tumultuous contingency experienced by the historical actors, let alone the ordinary by-standers, whose actions they are examining.

One perfectly obvious reason for the deceptively neat order of these accounts is precisely because they are "history." The events in question simply turned out one way rather than another, obscuring the fact that the participants likely had no idea how they would turn out and that, under slightly different circumstances, things might well have turned out very differently. As the saying has it, "For want of a nail, the shoe was lost; for want of a shoe the horse was lost; for want of a horse the rider was lost; for want a rider the message was lost; for want of the message the kingdom, was lost."

Knowing what in fact happened, unlike the participants, can't help but infect the story and drain much of its actual contingency. Think for a moment of someone who takes his or her own life. It becomes almost impossible for the suicide's friends and relatives not to rewrite the dead person's biography in a way that presages and accounts for the suicide. It is, of course, entirely possible that a brief chemical imbalance, a momentary panic, or an instant tragic insight may have led to the act, in which case rewriting the entire biography as leading up to suicide would be to misunderstand that life.

The natural impulse to create a coherent narrative to account for our own actions and lives, even when those lives and actions defy any coherent account, casts a retrospective order on acts that may have been radically contingent. Jean-Paul Sartre gives the hypothetical example of a man torn between the obligation of staying and caring for his ill mother or leaving for the front to defend his country. One could substitute the decision to go on strike or stay in the factory, the decision to join a demonstration, etc.) He can't make up his mind, but the day, like an on-rushing train, arrives, and he *must* do one thing or the other, though he still hasn't decided. Let's say he stays with his sick mother. The next day, Sartre writes, he will be able to tell himself and others why he is the kind of man who would chose to stay with his sick mother. He must, having acted, find a narrative that accounts for what he did. This does not, however, *explain* why he did what he did; rather, it retrospectively makes sense of—creates a satisfying narrative for—an act that cannot be explained in any other way.

The same could be said for the momentous, contingent events that have shaped history. Much history as well as popular imagination not only erases their contingency but implicitly attributes to historical actors intentions and a consciousness they could not possibly have had. The historical fact of the French Revolution has, understandably, recast virtually all of French eighteenth-century history as leading inexorably to 1789. The Revolution was not a single event but a process; it was contingent on weather, crop failures, and the geography and demography of Paris and Versailles far more than on the ideas scribbled by the *philosophes*. Those who stormed the Bastille to free prisoners and seize arms could not possibly have known (much less intended) that they would bring down the monarchy and aristocracy, let alone that they were participating in what later would come to be known as "the French Revolution."

Once a significant historical event is codified, it travels as a sort of condensation symbol and, unless we are very careful, takes on a false logic and order that does a grave injustice to how it was experienced at the time. The townsmen of Le

Chambon-sur-Lignon, now held up as moral exemplars, appear, more or less monolithically, as acting on Huguenot religious principles to aid the persecuted, when, as we saw, their bravery had more complex and instructive wellsprings. The Russian Revolution, the American Revolution, the Thirty Years' War (who knew in year five that it would last another twenty-five years?), the 1871 Commune of Paris, the U.S. civil rights movement, Paris in 1968, Solidarność in Poland, and any number of other complex events are subject to the same qualifications. Their radical contingency tends to be erased, the participants' consciousness is flattened and too often inoculated with a preternatural knowledge of how things turned out, and the tumult of different understandings and motives is stilled.

What "history" does to our understanding of events is akin to what a television broadcast does to our understanding of a basketball or ice hockey game. The camera is placed above and outside the plane of action, rather like a helicopter hovering above the action. The effect of this bird's-eye view is to distance the viewer from the play and apparently slow it down. Even then, lest the viewer miss a crucial shot or pass, actual slow motion is used to further slow the action and allow the viewer to see it in detail again and again. Combined, the bird's-eye perspective and slow motion make the players' moves seem deceptively easy to viewers, who might fantasize mastering such moves themselves. Alas, no actual player ever experiences the actual game from a helicopter or in slow motion. And when, rarely, the camera is placed at floor level and close to the action in real time, one finally appreciates the blinding speed and complexity of the game as the players experience it; the brief fantasy is instantly dispelled.

FRAGMENT 29
The Politics of Historical Misrepresentation

The confusion in seeing military causation is to confuse the parade
ground with the battle where it is a question of life and death.
Leo Tolstoy

The tendency to tidy up, simplify, and condense historical events is not just a natural human proclivity or something necessitated by schoolbook history but a political struggle with high stakes.

The Russian Revolution of 1917 was, like the French Revolution, a process in which the many and varied participants had no knowledge of the outcome. Those who have examined the process minutely agree on several things. They agree that the Bolsheviks played a negligible role in bringing it about; as Hannah Arendt put it, "The Bolsheviks found power lying in the street and picked it up."[4] The events of late October 1917 were marked by utter confusion and spontaneity. They agree that the collapse of the tsar's armies on the Austrian front and the subsequent rush home of soldiers to participate in spontaneous land seizures in the countryside were decisive in breaking tsarist power in rural Russia. They agree that the working class of Moscow and St. Petersburg, while discontented and militant, did not envision owning the factories. Finally, they agree that on the eve of the revolution, the Bolsheviks had precious little influence among workers and no influence whatever in the countryside.

Once the Bolsheviks had seized power, however, they began developing an account that wrote contingency, confusion, spontaneity, and the many other revolutionary groups out of the story. This new "just so" story emphasized the clair-voyance, determination, and power of the vanguard party. In keeping with the Leninist vision in *What Is to Be Done*, the Bolsheviks saw themselves as the prime animators of the his-torical outcome. Given the tenuousness with which they ruled from 1917 to 1921, the Bolsheviks had a powerful interest in moving the revolution out of the streets and into the museums and schoolbooks as soon as possible, lest the people decide to repeat the experience. The revolutionary process was "natural-ized" as a product of historical necessity, legitimating the "dic-tatorship of the proletariat."

The "official story" of the revolution was being elaborated almost before the real revolution was consummated. Just as Lenin's idea of the state (as well as of the revolution) resembled that of a well-oiled machine run from above with military pre-cision, so were subsequent revolutionary "reenactments" con-ducted along the same lines. Lunacharsky, the cultural impres-sario of early Bolshevism, devised a huge urban public theater depicting the revolution, with four thousand actors (mostly soldiers) following a choreographed script, canons, ships on the river, and a red sun in the east (simulated by searchlights) as civic instruction for 35,000 spectators. In public theater, literature, film, and history, the Bolsheviks expressed a vital interest in "packaging" the revolution in a way that elimi-nated all the contingency, variety, and cross purposes of the real revolution. After the generation that had experienced the revolution firsthand and could compare the script with its own experience had died, the official version tended to prevail.

Revolutions and social movements are, then, typically con-fected by a plurality of actors: actors with wildly divergent ob-jectives mixed with a large dose of rage and indignation, actors with little knowledge of the situation beyond their immediate ken, actors subject to chance occurrences (a rain shower, a rumor, a gunshot)—and yet the vector sum of this cacophony of events may set the stage for what later is seen as a revolution. They are rarely, if ever, the work of coherent organizations directing their "troops" to a determined objective, as the Leninist script would have it.[5]

The visual depiction of order and discipline is a staple of authoritarian stagecraft. Amid rural famine, urban hunger, and growing flight to the Chinese border, Kim Jong-Il managed to stage massive parades with tens of thousands of participants in a tableau meant to suggest a united populace moving in unison to the baton of the "Dear Leader" (fig. 6.1).

This form of theatrical bluster has a long lineage. It can be found in the early twentieth century in "mass exercises" organized by both socialist and right-wing parties in large stadiums as displays of power and discipline. The minutely coordinated movements of thousands of uniformed gymnasts, like those of a marching band in close-order drill, conveyed an image of synchronized power and, of course, of choreography scripted by a commanding but invisible orchestra conductor.

The pageantry of symbolic order is evident not only in public ceremonies such as coronations and May Day parades but in the very architecture of public spaces: squares, statuary, arches, and broad avenues. Buildings themselves are often designed to overawe the populace with their size and majesty. They often seem to function as a kind of shamanism, as a symbolic makeweight of order against a reality that is anything but orderly. Ceaușescu's Palace of the Parliament in Bucharest, 85 percent complete in 1989 when the regime fell, is a case in point. The "legislative assembly" resembled an opera house, with ringed balconies and a hydraulically lifted podium for Ceaușescu at

Figure 6.1.   North Korean military parade. Photograph © Reuters

the center. The building's six hundred clocks were all centrally controlled by a console in the president's suite.

A great deal of the symbolic work of official power is precisely to obscure the confusion, disorder, spontaneity, error, and improvisation of political power as it is in fact exercised, beneath a billiard-ball-smooth surface of order, deliberation, rationality, and control. I think of this as the "miniaturization of order." It is a practice we are all familiar with from the world of toys. The larger world of warfare, family life, machines, and wild nature is a dangerous reality that is beyond a child's control. Those worlds are domesticated by miniaturization in the form of toy soldiers, dollhouses, toy tanks and airplanes, model railroads, and small gardens. Much the same logic is at work in model villages, demonstration projects, model housing projects, and model collective farms. Experimentation on a small scale, where the consequences of failure are less catastrophic, is, of course, a prudent strategy for social innovation. More often, however, I suspect that such demonstrations are literally for "show," that they represent a substitute for more substantive change, and that they display a carefully tended micro-order designed in large part to mesmerize both rulers (self-hypnosis?) and a larger public with a Potemkin façade of centralized order. The greater the proliferation of these small "islands of order," the more one suspects they were erected to block one's view of an unofficial social order that is beyond the control of elites.

The condensation of history, our desire for clean narratives, and the need for elites and organizations to project an image of control and purpose all conspire to convey a false image of historical causation. They blind us to the fact that most revolutions are not the work of revolutionary parties but the precipitate of spontaneous and improvised action ("adventurism," in the Marxist lexicon), that organized social movements are usually the product, not the cause, of uncoordinated protests and demonstrations, and that the great emancipatory gains for human freedom have not been the result of orderly, institutional procedures but of disorderly, unpredictable, spontaneous action cracking open the social order from below.

Notes

PREFACE AND ACKNOWLEDGMENTS

1. Once in a great while one encounters an organization that combines some level of voluntary coordination while respecting and even encouraging local initiative. Solidarność in Poland under martial law and the Student Non-Violent Coordinating Committee during the civil rights movement in the United States are rare examples. Both came into existence only in the course of protest and struggle.
2. Frances Fox Piven and Richard A. Cloward, *Poor People's Movements: Why They Succeed, How They Fail* (New York: Vintage, 1978).
3. Milovan Djilas, *The New Class* (New York: Praeger, 1957).
4. Colin Ward, *Anarchy in Action* (London: Freedom Press, 1988), 14.
5. Pierre-Joseph Proudhon, *General Idea of the Revolution in the Nineteenth Century*, trans. John Beverly Robinson (London: Freedom Press, 1923), 293–94.
6. John Dunn, "Practising History and Social Science on 'Realist Assumptions,'" in *Action and Interpretation: Studies in the Philosophy of the Social Sciences*, ed. C. Hookway and P. Pettit (Cambridge: Cambridge University Press, 1979), 152, 168.

CHAPTER ONE
The Uses of Disorder and "Charisma"

1. Gramsci develops the concept of "hegemony" to explain the failure of universal suffrage to bring about working-class rule. See Antonio Gramsci, *The Prison Notebooks of Antonio Gramsci*, ed. and trans. Quentin Hoare and Geoffrey Nowell Smith (London: Lawrence and Wishart, 1971).
2. Taylor Branch, *Parting the Waters: America in the King Years, 1954–63* (New York: Simon and Schuster, 1988).
3. See R. R. Cobb, *The Police and the People: French Popular Protest, 1789–1820* (Oxford: Clarendon Press, 1970), 96–97.
4. Yan Yunxiang, conversation.
5. Kenneth Boulding, "The Economics of Knowledge and the Knowledge of Economics," *American Economic Review* 58, nos. 1/2 (March 1966): 8.

CHAPTER TWO
Vernacular Order, Official Order

1. E. F. Schumacher, *Small Is Beautiful: Economics As If People Mattered* (New York: Harper, 1989), 117.
2. Edgar Anderson, *Plants, Man, and Life* (Boston: Little, Brown, 1952) 140–41.

CHAPTER THREE
The Production of Human Beings

1. Colin Ward, *Anarchy in Action* (London: Freedom Press, 1988), 92. The playground examples are all drawn from the introduction to Ward's chapter 10, pp. 89–93.
2. Alexis de Tocqueville, *Democracy in America*, trans. George Lawrence (New York: Harper-Collins, 1988), 555.
3. Stanley Milgram, *Obedience to Authority: An Experimental View* (New York: Harper-Collins, 1974); Philip G. Zimbardo, *The Lucifer Effect: How Good People Turn Evil* (New York: Random House, 2008).

4. See, for example, http://www.telegraph.co.uk/news/uknews/1533248/Is-this-the-end-of-the-road-for-traffic-lights.html.

CHAPTER FOUR
Two Cheers for the Petty Bourgeoisie

1. R. H. Tawney, *Religion and the Rise of Capitalism* (Harmondsworth: Penguin, 1969), 28.
2. Paul Averich, *Kronstadt 1921* (Princeton, NJ: Princeton University Press, 1970), 66.
3. Vaisberg, speaking in 1929, and quoted in R. W. Davies, *The Socialist Offensive: The Collectivization of Russian Agriculture, 1929–1930* (London: Macmillan, 1980), 175.
4. A. V.Chayanov, *The Theory of Peasant Economy*, ed. Daniel Thorner, trans. Basile Kerblay and R. E. F. Smith (Homewood, IL: Richard Irwin for the American Economic Association, 1966, originally published in Russian in 1926).
5. Henry Stephens Randall, "Cultivators," in *The Life of Thomas Jefferson*, vol. 1, 1858, p. 437.
6. Barrington Moore, Jr., *Injustice: The Social Basis of Obedience* (Armonk, NY: M. E. Sharpe, 1978).
7. Robert E. Lane, *Political Ideology: Why the American Common Man Believes What He Does* (Glencoe, IL: Free Press, 1962).
8. Steven H. Hahn, *The Roots of Southern Populism: Yeoman Farmers and the Transformation of the Georgia Upcountry* (Oxford: Oxford University Press, 1984).
9. See, e.g., Alf Ludke, "Organizational Order or Eigensinn? Workers' Privacy and Workers' Politics," in *Rites of Power, Symbolism, Ritual and Politics since the Middle Ages*, ed. Sean Wilentz (Philadelphia: University of Pennsylvania Press, 1985), 312–44; Miklos Haraszti, *Worker in a Worker's State* (Harmondsworth: Penguin, 1977); and Ben Hamper, *Rivet Head: Tales from the Assembly Line* (Boston: Little, Brown, 1991).
10. M. J. Watts and P. Little, *Globalizing Agro-Food* (London: Routledge, 1997).
11. See, e.g., the assertion by Michel Crozier that even within large bureaucratic organizations, the key to behavior is "the insistence of the

individual of his own autonomy and his refusal of all dependence relationships." *The Bureaucratic Phenomenon* (Chicago: University of Chicago Press, 1964), 290.

12. Barrington Moore, *The Social Origins of Dictatorship and Democracy* (Boston: Beacon Press, 1966). See also E. P. Thompson's magnificent *The Making of the English Working Class* (New York: Vintage, 1966).

13. There are other social contributions of the petty bourgeoisie that are noteworthy no matter one's location on the political spectrum. Historically, petty trade and petty production have been the key engine of market integration. If there is a good or service that is in short supply somewhere and that will therefore command a higher return, the petty bourgeoisie will usually find a way to move it where it is needed. For the likes of Milton Friedman and market fundamentalists, the petty bourgeoisie are doing "God's work." They operate in a setting of nearly perfect competition; their agility and speed in responding to small movements in supply and demand come close to the utopian vision of perfect competition in neoclassical economics. Their profit margins are slim, they often fail, and yet their aggregate activity contributes to Pareto-optimum outcomes. The petty bourgeoisie, in general, come reasonably close to this idealization. They provide needed goods and services at competitive prices with an alacrity that larger and slower-footed firms are unable to match.

14. I write "perhaps" here because there was, at mid-century, a research culture in large firms such as AT&T (Bell Labs), DuPont, and IBM that suggests that large firms are not necessarily inherently hostile to innovation.

15. Jance Jacobs, *The Death and Life of Great American Cities* (New York: Vintage, 1961).

CHAPTER FIVE
For Politics

1. "Atlanta's Testing Scandal Adds Fuel to U.S. Debate," *Atlanta Journal Constitution*, July 13, 2011.

2. C. A. E. Goodhart, "Monetary Relationships: A View from Thread-needle Street," *Papers in Monetary Economics* (Reserve Bank of Australia, 1975).

3. Theodore Porter, *Trust in Numbers: The Pursuit of Objectivity in Science and Public Life* (Princeton, NJ: Princeton University Press, 1995), 43.

4. Lorraine Daston, "Objectivity and the Escape from Perspective," *Social Studies of Science* 22 (1992): 597–618.

5. The term "meritocracy" was coined in the late 1940s by the Englishman Michael Young in his dystopian fantasy, *The Rise of the Meritocracy, 1870–2033: An Essay on Education and Inequality* (London: Thames & Hudson, 1958), which mused on the disadvantages, for the working class, of a ruling elite chosen on the basis of IQ scores.

6. Porter, *Trust in Numbers*, 194.

7. Where do we draw the line between justified quantification, which seeks to achieve transparency, objectivity, democratic control, and egalitarian social outcomes, and metastasized quantification, which replaces and indeed stifles political discussions about the proper course of public policy?

We surely cannot conclude that all official uses of audit methods are wrong and foolish. Rather, we need to find ways to distinguish between sensible and dangerous uses of numbers. When confronted by audit or quantitative indices, we should ask ourselves a few questions. I would suggest asking questions that respond to the concerns I raised earlier in my discussion, namely, the presence or lack of construct validity, the possibility of "antipolitics," and the colonization or feedback danger. Thus, we as citizens should ask ourselves:

a. What is the relation between the proposed quantitative index and the construct—the thing in the world—it is supposed to measure? (For example, does the SAT accurately represent a student's aptitude, or more broadly, whether he or she deserves to go to college?)

b. Is a political question being hidden or evaded under the guise of quantification? (For example, did the hamlet

evaluation point system and the body count method ob-
fuscate the American debate about whether the Vietnam
War was wise or indeed winnable?)

c. What are the possibilities for colonization or subversion
of the index, such as misreporting, feedback effects, or
the prejudicing of other substantive goals? (Does reliance
on the SSCI in American universities lead to the publica-
tion of lousy articles or the phenomenon of "citation
rings"?)

In short, I am not proposing an attack on quantitative methods, whether in the academy or in the polity. But we do need to de-
mystify and desacralize numbers, to insist that they cannot always
answer the question we are posing. And we do need to recognize
debates about allocation of scarce resources for what they are—
politics—and what they are not—technical decisions. We must
begin to ask ourselves whether the use of quantification in a particular context is likely to advance or hinder political debate, and
whether it is likely to achieve or undermine or our political goals.

CHAPTER SIX
Particularity and Flux

1. François Rochat and Andre Modigliani, "The Ordinary Quality of
Resistance: From Milgram's Laboratory to the Village of Le Chambon," *Journal of Social Issues* 51, no. 3 (1995): 195–210.
2. The Holocaust Museum in Washington, D.C., recognizes the
power of particularity by giving every visitor a card with an individual photograph of a Jew whose particular fate they learn only at
the end of the visit.
3. Most of these plaques were not a state initiative but were created by
small groups of German citizens who insisted on the importance
of marking the local history of Nazism in the collective historical
memory. While they are less moving on the whole than the Münster exhibition, they compare favorably with the United States,
where one looks largely in vain for memorial reminders such as
"Slave auctions were held on this site," "Let us remember 'Wounded

Knee' and 'The Trail of Tears,'" or "Here were conducted the infamous Tuskegee Experiments."

4. Hannah Arendt, *On Revolution* (New York: Viking, 1965), 122.

5. Lenin's writings are complex in this respect, sometimes celebrating spontaneity, but, as a general matter, he saw the "masses" as raw power, rather like a fist, and the vanguard party as the "brain," as the general staff deploying the power of the masses to best advantage.

Acknowledgments

At Princeton University Press, Fred Appel, with exemplary patience, aided and abetted my freestyle experiment with form here, and exercised the kind of editorial care and advice I thought had disappeared from contemporary publishing. His colleagues Sarah David and Deborah Tegarden generously

Index

abolitionism, xviii. *See also* slavery

absenteeism, xx

abstractness, 34

abstract principles, 131, 132

Abuja, 45, 141

academy, quantitative measures of productivity in, 105–11. *See also* citation indices; education

accountants, chartered, 121

adaptability, 65–66

administration, xiii, 120, 127; and models, 44–45

adventure playgrounds, 57–59, 60. *See also* play

aesthetics, xxiii, 7, 45, 47, 99

affirmative action, 123

African American church, 23

African Americans, xiv, 25, 26, 104. *See also* civil rights movement

agribusiness, 87, 93–94

Agricultural Adjustment Act, 17

agriculture, 42, 48–51; and Andean potato cultivation, 39–40;

depletion vs. development of soil in, 69; and irrigation, 36; plantation, 37, 38–40, 41, 87; and proletarian production crops, 48; scientific, 37–40, 48–49; and share-cropping system, 92; smallholder, 87; and vernacular knowledge, 33–34, 48–51; Western, 48–49. *See also* farming

airplanes, manufacture of, 36

Aksoy, Mehmet, *Memorial for the Unknown Deserter*, 8

almanacs, 33

Amazon, 38–40

American Civil War, 8–10

American Revolution, 136

anarchism/anarchists, 5, 80; calisthenics for, 1–7; and democracy, 121; and dignity and autonomy of small property, 94; and Global South, xi; and mutuality without hierarchy, 122;

anarchism/anarchists *(cont)*; and
petty bourgeoisie, 85; and
praxis, xii; principles of, xii
anarchist squint, xii–xvi, xvii
ancien regime, x
Anderson, *Edgar, Plants, Man,
and Life,* 49–53
Andes, potato cultivation in,
39–40
anonymity, 8, 10–11, 12, 13, 76,
97
anticolonial movements, 94
antipolitics, 111, 122, 126, 127,
147n7. *See also* politics
anti-Semitism, 86, 129. *See also*
Jews
architecture, 34, 43–44, 45, 47,
139
archives, 12–13
Arendt, Hannah, 131, 137
Argentina, xxv
artisans, 85; autonomy of, 95; as
core of working-class movements, 95; knowledge of, 68;
as political thinkers, xxiii;
production by, 34, 36; as small
property owners, 88; and
struggles for equality, 96; and
vernacular, 40
Arts and Humanities Citation
Index, 108, 112
assembly line. *See* factories; industry; workers
asylums, 79
AT&T Bell Labs, 146n14
attrition, index of, 117
audience, 23–28, 144n3

audits, 147n7; and corporations,
126–27; and cost-benefit analysis, 123; and education, 71,
116, 117, 127; and Enron, 118;
and financial collapse of 2008,
119; and McNamara, 118;
Porter on, 125; and quantitative measures, 115, 121
authoritarianism, xix, xxi, xxiii, 16,
77–78, 79, 139
autonomy: and agribusiness,
93–94; and anarchism, xxiii;
and Andean farmers, 40; of
artisans, 95; and assembly line,
92–93; and authoritarian-
ism, 78, 79; and compulsory
universal education, 71; and
contract farming, 93–94; and
Crozier, 145n11; and Emdrup
playground, 60; expansion of,
80; and industrial workers, 91–
92; and patriarchal family, 77;
and petty bourgeoisie, 85; and
small property, 85, 89, 90, 94;
for subordinate classes, 88–89.
See also independence

Bakunin, Mikhail, xi–xii, xv, xxv
Bangkok, housing in, 59–60
banks, 53, 77, 87. *See also* World
Bank
bard, medieval, 26–27, 28, 29
Bastille, storming of, 135
Battle in Seattle, xix
beauty, 124. *See also* aesthetics
Bell Labs, 146n14
Berlin, Isaiah, xxv

Berlin Wall, 1, 2, 6, 46
big box stores, 99
Big Mac sandwich, 35
Big Ten universities, 107
biography, 134–35
black bloc strategy, xix
body counts, 117, 147n7
body parts, international trade
    in, xv
Bolshevik Revolution, 86
Bolsheviks, 137–38
bond rating agencies, 119
border states, 9
Boulding, Kenneth, 29
boycotts, 17
Branch, Taylor, 23–25
Brasilia, 45
Brazil, 38–40, 94
Brecht, Bertolt, 6
Brown, Stuart, 64–65
Bukharin, Nikolai, 86–87
bureaucracies, 85, 88, 145n11
Burma, x
business conglomerates, 87

call-and-response tradition, 23
campaign contributions, xvi
capitalism: and crisis beginning in
    2008, xvi; and Global South,
    xi; and petty bourgeoisie, 84,
    86, 87, 94–95; and proletariat,
    95
Caterpillar Corporation, 46
Catherine the Great, 118
Ceau&#015f;escu, Nicolae,
    139–40
Central America, 49

ceremonial space, 41
charisma, relationship of, 22–29
children, xv, 46, 57–59, 60, 77
China, x, xi, xv, 27–28, 72, 90–91
Chuang Tzu, 16, 61
citation indices, 108–11, 112–15,
    122, 147n7. See also academy
citation rings, 114, 148n7
cities, 32–33, 41–45, 47. See also
    urban planning
citizens/citizenship, xiv, 70, 78,
    80, 89, 90, 91, 121–22
civil disobedience, 15, 16. See also
    dissent; protests
civil engineering, 41
civil rights, xix, 16, 20, 88. See also
    freedom
civil rights movement, xviii, 17,
    21–22, 25, 136, 143n1
civil war, 16
Cloward, Richard A., xviii
Cold War, xi, 21, 95
collective action, 13, 14
collective farms, 87
collectivism, xi
collectivization, x, 91
colonialism, 31, 53
commercialization, 56
commercial regulations, 55
commercial retail space, 41
commodities, xvi, xxii, 36, 37,
    42, 56
commons, 92
Commune of Paris of 1871, 136
communism, xi, xxi, 86
concentration camps, 79

Confederate States of America, 8–10, 92

Congress, 21

Congress on Racial Equality, 21

conscription, xiv, xx, 9, 10, 34, 70

construct validity, 147n7

consumers, fabrication of, 55

contagion effect, 14–15

contingency, 31, 134–36, 137, 138

convalescent homes, 73–76

cooperation, xii, xxi–xxii, xxiii

coordination, xxi, 14–15, 21, 36, 81, 82

corporate managers, 118–19

corporations, 55, 87, 127. *See also* firms

cost-benefit analysis, xxii, 111, 123–25, 126

courts, 12, 34. *See also* law

Crozier, Michel, 145–46n11

Cultural Revolution, 27–28

culture, 17, 56

currency, standardization of, 55

custom, 16, 54

Danvers High School, Massachusetts, 102

Daston, Lorraine, 120

Davos World Economic Forum, 84

debate, xiii; elimination of, 119, 121, 122, 123, 127, 147n7; and quantification, 148n7

decisions, 121, 124, 125, 126, 127, 134–35

democracy: and audit society, 127; capacity for, 70; and capacity of citizenry to grow, 121–22; as commodity, xvi; debate in, 121, 122; disruptions in name of, xviii; and dissent, 16–21; and educational opportunity, 123; and extra-institutional disorder, 19; and inequality, xvi; and Jefferson, 79–80, 89, 100; and life of subservience, 78; and meritocracy, 111, 120–21; moral high ground of, xviii–xix; overthrow of representative, 20; and petty bourgeoisie, 87; and protest movements, xvii; purpose of representative, 16; and quantitative measures of quality, 119; and state's emancipatory role, xiv

demonstrations, xvii, 16, 18, 21, 22. *See also* protests

Department of Defense, 106

Department of Education, 104

desegregation, xviii

desertion, xx, 5–7, 9–11, 12

development studies, xi

Dickens, Charles, *Hard Times*, 70, 101

Diggers, 94

dignity, 89, 94

discipline, 77, 139

disobedience, 7, 8, 10, 11

disruption: and civil rights movement, 21; and democratic political change, 17; and emancipa-

elites *(cont)*: and social science,
xxiii. *See also* charisma, relationship of
Emdrup, Denmark, playground
in, 57–58, 59, 60
employment, 111
enclosure, bills of, 12
engineers, 34, 46, 70, 120, 121,
123
England, poaching in, 11. *See also*
Great Britain
English, as second language, 104
English Civil War, 94
English monarchy, 11
English nobility, 11
Enron Corporation, 105, 118–19
entertainment, 41
epidemics, control of, 36
Europe, 10
evil, banality of, 131
eyes on the street, 98–99

factories, 18, 47, 79, 92; and
artisanal production, 36; labor
force of, 85, 95; and Owens,
108; and public schools, 70, 71;
and schools, 103; task environment of, 65; workers in, 77. *See
also* industry; workers
facts, 119–20
families, 19, 76, 77–78, 79, 80, 87,
88, 90
farmers: and Bukharin, 87; and
Jefferson, 89, 100; landowning,
79–80; peasant, 77; tenant, 77,
85, 89, 90

farming: contract, 93–94; large
vs. smallholder, 36. *See also*
agriculture
farms, model, 45, 141
fascism, xix
federal voting registrars, 21
feedback effects, 147n7
fence laws, 92
feudalism, 86
financial collapse of 2008, xvi, 119
financial mobility, 72
fingerprints, 34
Finland, 104
firms, 96, 100, 118–19, 146n14.
See also corporations
First International Congress of the
Petite Bourgeoisie, 84
First Republic, 10
foot-dragging, xx, 16
footpaths, 15–16, 61
Ford, Henry, 35, 38–40
Ford Foundation, 106
Fordism, 35, 66
Fordlandia, 38–40
Ford River Rouge Complex, 39,
40, 68, 92
foreign loans and aid, 55
forestry, scientific, 37–38, 41, 42
fragging, 11
fragments, as term, xxiv–xxv
France, 16, 54, 121; anarchist
workers of, xxv; École des Ponts
et Chausées, 123; education in,
72; taxation in, 115; universal
citizenship of revolutionary,
70; Vichy, 129, 130
Franco, Francisco, 130

impartiality, 123, 126
income distribution, 18
independence: and authoritarianism, 78; and contract farming,
93–94; and industrialized
proletariat, 91; and Jeffersonian
democracy, 79, 80, 89, 100; of
judgment, 79, 81–83; and land
ownership, 91; and patriarchal
family, 77; and petty bourgeoisie, 94; and slavery, 92; and
small property, 89, 90, 91, 96;
for subordinate classes, 88–89;
and village class system, 90. *See
also* autonomy
India, x
Indonesia, x
industrial associations, 84
industrializing society, 70
industrial proletariat, 91
Industrial Revolution, 77, 94
industry, 35, 86, 87. *See also* factories; workers
inequalities, xi, xiv–xvi, 19
infrapolitics, xx
innovation, 96, 146n14
institutions: adaptability and
breadth of, 65; as authoritarian, 77, 79; caring, 73–76;
disruption of, xvii; and dissent,
17–18; efficiency vs. human
results of, 67; failure of, 19; as
hierarchical, 77, 79; modifica-
tion of, 61; and North Atlantic
nation-state, 53–54; opposition, xvii–xviii; and protest
movements, xvii; and public

sphere, 80; and purposes and
talents of inhabitants, 60–61;
and scientific design, xiii; as
sclerotic, xvii; shaping by, 76–
80; task environment of, 65;
threat to, xviii; total, 79; for
unruly protest and anger, 20
insubordination, 7–22. *See also*
dissent
intelligence, 71, 73, 120, 127
Intelligence Quotient, 126
International Monetary Fund,
xix, 55
international organizations, 55
Irish democracy, 14
Islamabad, 45, 141
Italy, xxv, 54, 130
Ivy League schools, 107, 116–17
Iwo Jima Memorial (U. S. Marine
Corps War Memorial), Washington, D.C., 62–63, 64

Jacobs, Jane, 42–43, 47, 98, 99
Japan, 72
jaywalking, 4–5
Jefferson, Thomas, 89, 100. *See
also* democracy
Jews, 86, 129–33, 148n2
justice, 4, 5, 22

Kampuchea, xi
Kang, Mia, 102
Kaplan, Stanley, 116
Kennedy, John, 21
Kennedy, Robert, 21
Khmer Rouge, xi
Kim, Jong-Il, 139

peasants *(cont)*; land ownership for, 91; lawbreaking by, 11–13; and Mao Zedong, xi; and Mexican Revolution, 94; and petty bourgeoisie, 85; as political thinkers, xxiii; and radicalism, 95; and revolutions, 91; smallholding, 88, 89–90, 96, 99; and struggles for equality, 96; suppression of, x–xi; and wars of national liberation, x

peddlers, 85

Pentagon, 117

Peter the Great, 141

petition, rights to, 88

petty bourgeoisie, 84–100; and citizenship, 90; and dream of independence, 94; economic role in invention and innovation, 96; and industrial proletariat, 91; Marxist contempt for, 86–88; Marx's contempt for, 94–95; and meaning of property, 90; and revolutionary ferment, 90; as shopkeepers, 97–100; social functions of, 94–96, 146n13; social services by, 98–100

philosophes, 135

photography, 34

Piven, Frances Fox, xviii

plantation agriculture, 37, 38–40, 41, 87

plantation economy, 92

play, 57–59, 63–65, 93

Pletz, Germany, 1–2, 3, 5

ploughmen, 85

poaching, xx, 11, 12, 13–14, 16

police, 12, 34, 99

political capitals, 140–41

politicians, 28, 29, 44–45. *See also* leaders, and followers

politics, xvii, 17, 125, 140; and anarchist squint, xii; and change from below, xxi; and cost-benefit analysis, 125; extra-institutional, xx; and historical misrepresentation, 137–41; and institutionalized protest, 20; and lawbreaking and disruption, 17–18; and measures of quality, 111; mutuality and learning in, 111; parliamentary, 17; partisan, 120; privileged influence in, 17; and quantitative assessment, 121–28; as replaced by administration, xiii; routine, 18, 19; and scientific modernists, 120; study of, xvii; and urban planning, 41; and warning signs of unrest, 13

pollution, 36

Pompidou, Georges, xviii

poor people, xv, 19, 28, 45, 79, 92

populism, xxiii

Porter, Theodore, 116, 125

postmodern era, 42

potatoes, cultivation of, 39–40

Potemkin, Grigory, 118

Potemkin façade, 141

poultry-raising, 93

prisons, 71, 78, 79

professions, 85, 121, 125

proletariat, x, xiii, 77, 86, 91, 94, 95, 138